praise
Feisty: A Memoir

"Incredibly moving and sweetly honest, this beautiful memoir has a light touch with a bright flame. *Feisty* traces the lines of the female movement through the nooks and crannies of Jean's experiences—divinely feminine and full of rumbling urgency. A powerful female tale—radical in its dignified honesty and powerful in its scope, while remaining sweetly intimate."

LIZ TIGELAAR   Executive producer of the series *Life Unexpected, Little Fires Everywhere*, and *Tiny Beautiful Things*

"In short chapters, with photographs, poetry, and even a recipe, Jean Peelen shares her life as a nascent to fully-emerged feminist, as a wife and mother, as a civil rights lawyer—all with the joy in being human firstly. . . . My wish would be for young people to read this work, to witness history, the lengthy and exhausting and joyous path others have broken. "

ALISON ACHESON   Author of *Dance Me to the End: Ten Months and Ten Days with ALS*

"Peelen's eighty-plus years draw a portrait of a woman's life that is simultaneously familiar and unknown, intimidating and exhilarating, especially the price women pay in pursuit of self, freedom, and not least of all, joy."

JILL NELSON   Journalist and author of *Volunteer Slavery: My Authentic Negro Experience* and *Let's Get It On*

"There is a world of wisdom in this little book. It is one of the funniest and saddest things I have ever read and full of hard-won humanity. It is brief only because there is not a wasted word, but any woman who was ever a child, a daughter, a mother, a sister, a schoolgirl, a citizen, was married or divorced, in fact, who was ever born will find echoes of the journey in this magical account of growing up and finally growing old."

JANE CAMPBELL   Author of *Cat Brushing*

"In sixty-five brush strokes, Jean Peelen paints a portrait of her own life, but also a landscape of the socioeconomic change experienced by women who came of age with the women's liberation movement of the 1970s. Readers will love the honesty and humor with which young Jean asks, and mature Jean answers, 'What do *I* want?'"

HEATHER NEWTON   Author of *Under the Mercy Trees* and *McMullen Circle*

feisty

feisty

a memoir in little pieces

JEAN PEELEN

BOLD STORY PRESS

CHEVY CHASE, MD

Bold Story Press, Chevy Chase, MD 20815
www.boldstorypress.com

This book is a memoir and it reflects the author's present
recollections of experiences over time.

First edition: September 2023

Library of Congress Control Number: 2023907567

ISBN: 978-1-954805-50-7 (paperback)
ISBN: 978-1-954805-51-4 (ebook)

Author photo by Joyce Kramer

Photos are from the author's personal collection unless otherwise noted:

Page 68 Used with permission from Dorjän Scott

Page 95 Used with permission from Gloria's Foundation
Archives and Ray Bald, 1973

Page 98 Ronald Grant Archive / Alamy Stock Photo

Page 129 "Justice Clarence Thomas," by Cknight70, https://www.flickr.com/
photos/cknight70/8681466634/in/photolist-ee9Mzd-ym4VXb-2m6TCFE-
8gDbzJ-7488A2-75dBqR-G6ieFp-7tx2HS-8Zbs4H-8AAGFW-8ZetrU-8ZetaJ-
2ixmFm-2aqPMHU-9rmyAZ-bsGHRk-2kxQm9w-2ntKunb-7rpAdG-2hBJ78H-
2jaEnr5-G6iehi-2nunzon-2oru1Sq-iscpNv-2mi1TPP-jcePd6-2noXYcX-
2opEZKU-2mMePDJ-zUNCgy-2oru27i-2osCjMD-7pPF2U-axBMyq-A88N4V-
AAw8WC-9E6tYJ-9E3zsp-zByrF5-9E6tKQ-2kJHmJG-Af5Pj4-9E3AoP-4YbmxW-
qbJeru-Av3K83-GCEm4f-AHp28o-ABoTnd, licensed under CC BY 2.0

Page 186 Used with permission from Eli Lilly and Company

Page 193 Source: Library of Congress. New York World-
Telegram & Sun Collection, Author: Fred Palumbo, World
Telegram staff photographer. Restored by Adam Cuerden.

Printed in the United States of America
10 9 8 7 6 5 4 3 2 1

To the badass women who opened our eyes
and opened the door.

contents

CONTENTS

STIRRING

PREPARING

CONTENTS

BLOOMING

MOVING INWARD

GOING OUT WITH A BANG

CONTENTS

PURE PLEASURE

COSTS

AND THE BEAT GOES ON

The world wanted me to nest.
I wanted to fly.

A FEMALE CHILD

1

hello yellow

1946
age 5

"WAS I REALLY born yellow?'

My mother sighs, weary of my asking. "I've told you this story so many times."

"Yellow?"

"Yes. You were born yellow."

"Bright yellow? Like a banana?"

"No, not that bright, light yellow."

"But babies aren't supposed to be yellow, right?"

"Right." I wait.

"The doctor said you were jaundiced, and they might need to replace all your blood."

I love that sentence. I could have had somebody else's blood. I feel the goosebumps on my arms.

"Why didn't they do it? Why didn't they change my blood?"

"You just got better by all by yourself. The yellow faded away."

"What did the doctor say then?" I ask. This is my very favorite part.

"The doctor said, 'She is one feisty kid!'"

the raft

1948
age 7

"JUST SWIM THERE, hang on, get your breath, then swim back to shore. No getting up on the raft! There's a bunch of big boys on the raft."

"OK."

I high-step through the shallow water. This is the first time my mother has allowed me to go past the safety ropes. Finally! I'm already seven, and I've been swimming since last summer and I'm good at it.

I'm almost to the raft and not tired at all. My parents are both sitting on the beach on the plaid blanket, probably watching me. My mother's eagle eye is always alert for the breaking of rules.

I reach the raft and grab the rope on the side. I'm proud of myself. I wave.

"Get out of here, kid!"

It's the biggest boy. I think he's in the fifth grade.

"I don't have to."

"You're a wimpy kid."

"I'm not wimpy. I'm as brave as you!"

"Then climb up here."

I pull my body up halfway out of the water and throw one leg over the top of the raft to get all the way up. The boys start rocking the raft to make it harder. They are laughing. I am hanging on but trying to climb, determined to make it.

Every time the boys rock, the raft tips further. When my side is low, I am dunked underwater. I'm going to hang on until they stop. They'll see I won't quit.

Suddenly, the raft flips all the way over. I am underneath it, underwater. I hadn't had time to take a breath. I need to breathe. My legs are churning but going nowhere. My head hits the raft. I can feel my heart beating so hard it is going to burst from my body. I grope around the raft above, feeling for the edge. I can't get out. I am going to explode if I don't breathe.

A hand grabs my arm and pulls me out from under the raft and into the fresh air. It is my father. I can breathe. He pulls me to him with one arm, his other holding on to the overturned raft. I hang on to him, shaking.

3

_____

what i wanted

_____

1949
age 8

THERE AREN'T ANY cowboys in New Jersey.

Even so, every night I slide out of bed quietly so as not to wake my sister. I put on the white half-mask I got for Halloween and stand at the end of my bed facing the closet where the bad guys live. I let my hands drift over my pretend six-guns, readying to shoot.

It's a facedown. I walk slowly, leather holster slung around my hips, down the dusty street toward the bad guy.

"You sure you want to do this, pardner?" I ask, my voice soft but powerful.

He cowers at the sight of me and my guns. I fast draw my guns. The bad guy surrenders, hands up.

I perform this theater over and over, never tiring of the look of surprise on the bad guys' faces and the feeling of power flowing through me.

I learned everything I know about being a hero cowboy from the four o'clock Western.

Good guy line: "Come on cowboy, you know that's not the right thing to do."

Bad guy line: "We'll ambush them in the canyon."

Cowboys never seem afraid and never seem to doubt the outcome, while the bad guys are always wrong about it. The good guys in the movies never draw first. They wait for the bad guy to make the first move, then beat him to the draw. I'm not sure it is a great idea to wait for the bad guy to draw first. I would want the advantage. I think I can draw first and still be a good guy.

I could be the first New Jersey cowboy.

4

the breaking of rules

1950
age 9

MY MOTHER WILL be calling me for dinner soon. I wonder where my friends are. We usually play dodgeball or something in the schoolyard, but no one is around this afternoon.

The school janitor comes to a doorway. I see him around the school almost every day and always say "hi," but have never talked to him.

"Hi."

"Hi," he returns. He is smoking a cigarette.

"Can I come in?" I ask. I know going into school after hours is not allowed.

"Sure."

I leave my bike leaning against the brick wall and follow him inside. Empty and quiet, the school is an entirely different place.

I walk from room to room, the janitor following. Here is the first-graders' room; there is the nurse's office. I'm a little worried to be where I'm not allowed, but it is exciting to see my school this way. It almost isn't my school anymore. Now, after school hours, it is the janitor's place.

I hear kids laughing outside. I feel the weight of breaking the rules. "I should go soon."

"Want to see where I work first?"

The janitor heads for the stairs to the basement. The basement, a place of mystery, a place of clanking pipes. Going to the basement is the ultimate in forbidden actions.

I take a deep breath. "Sure."

The janitor leads the way down the stone steps. It is darker here than upstairs. I don't like the creepy cold feeling wrapping around me. I won't be here long, just look and then out.

He opens a door and steps into a room, beckoning me to follow. "This is my office." I look around. It is a dark, crowded little space. There is no desk, just an old couch and what looks like parts of machines and junk. The janitor sits on the couch. "Come here," he says, opening his arms.

My heart flutters. Something is wrong. I take a small step toward him, suddenly aware he is a tall man. Even sitting down, he is my height. He pulls me toward him. "I just want to show you how much I like you," he says.

We are face-to-face. I have never really looked at his face. I have never seen the scars, the white whiskers on his cheeks, the eyebrows that pull together, the look in his eyes. The look is the worst. He is looking at me but isn't looking at me. He is seeing something else. He closes his eyes.

Everything freezes. Breath, sight, hearing seem to disappear, to be unavailable. I stand in the circle of his arms. Something is horribly wrong, but I don't know what it is. This is not right.

It is not right.

"I want to love you," he whispers.

He takes my hand. "Come feel this." He moves my hand to his lap and holds it to his body. I don't know what is there. I feel a moving lump under his clothes. Terror grips me. "Feel this. Doesn't that feel good?" He presses my hand to his body. He rubs and rubs with my hand. With his other hand, he pulls me all the way to him. He moves my hand faster and faster. He shakes and groans.

 For a minute there is silence.

"Do you want to touch me?" he asks, moving my hand to his waistband.

"No," I whisper. "No."

"Can I touch you?"

"No. No. I have to go home."

"Don't tell anyone."

 He releases me. I pull back and run out of his room and up the stairs. I'm worried he might come after me. I run out of the school and across the street to my house. My legs churn and my heart pounds in my ears. I run into the house and up the stairs to my room. I curl up on my bed, shaking. I don't know what just happened. All I know is that I had been disobedient and went into the school and made something bad happen.

 I don't tell anyone.

it's not over yet

1950
age 9

THE JANITOR COMES into my classroom to fix the radiator. As he passes behind my desk in the back corner of the room, he runs his hand across the back of my neck. I freeze. I look up at the teacher, but she is talking to someone in the front row. I am trembling and can't seem to breathe normally. I keep my eyes on my desk until he is gone. It takes a while to feel OK again. After that day, the janitor seems to find reasons to be in the classroom, and every time, he touches my neck. From the moment he comes in, my body goes rigid, dreading his touch. Why doesn't anybody notice that he comes in this room a lot? Why doesn't the teacher notice him touching my neck? I could ask the teacher to change my seat, but I can't think of a reason to give her. I don't want to be in school anymore.

Today, he is waiting in the little side entryway I use to leave school because it is closest to my house. I turn to run but the door has closed behind me and he is between me and the outside door. He pulls me to him, rubbing his body on me. I pretend I am not there. I pretend I don't feel anything he is doing. I see myself running home to safety. Again, his breathing gets heavy and faster and faster. He shakes, hugs me tight, then lets me go.

"Don't tell anyone."

the lesson

1950
age 9

ON THE WAY home from school today, a second-grader who lives two houses down from us says to me, "The janitor touched me funny today. It was weird."

"He did that to me, too," I reply. "Don't tell anyone."

Within an hour, my house is filled with people. My parents, the police chief, the school principal, my teacher, and my neighbor's mother and father crowd our little living room. I don't know why all these people are here. My mother is sitting in the far corner of the room. My father says, "It's OK, honey, the chief just wants to talk to you about the janitor."

It's done. I am found out, and there is no way to get out of it.

The police chief starts asking me questions. My mother is still across the room, not looking at me, staring down at her hands. I feel afraid, embarrassed, and horribly guilty that I have caused all of this. I can't meet anybody's eyes. I want to disappear. I have shamed my parents.

"Did the janitor force you into the school?" the chief asks.

"No."

"Then why did you go in?"

"Because he asked me to."

The lie was said. The lie was in my living room. "He asked me to come in."

My father says the janitor will be sent to prison or a mental institution. I know I caused this. It is clear to me that I am a troublemaker and a liar, and no one should ever trust me again.

latin club

1955
age 14

I'M SECRETLY ATTRACTED to the dropout kids: the boys with their ducktail haircuts, sideburns, and black leather jackets; the girls with their shorter-than-proper skirts and heavily hair-sprayed French twists. Most of the high school world is black and white, but the dropout kids are technicolor. I watch the boys loll against their cars, smoking and flirting with the girls. They don't care what anyone thinks of them. They are in their own world. I love that "don't give a damn" attitude, but there is something just too dangerous for me about them. For one thing, I don't know what these kids do when they're not in school. Maybe they do illegal things. What I know for sure is these kids will live here, right here, the rest of their lives. There is no way out.

There is no adventure, no learning. I can't risk getting involved with them.

It's the smart kids I admire. They exhibit qualities I want: poise, confidence, assurance about who they are. They are from families who go to college. No one in my family has been to college. All my friends are pretty much like me. We aren't even a group. We are the middle people: bland, lower middle class, sale-rack clothes, untraveled, inexperienced, insecure.

I hang out near the smart kids a lot and just listen. I'm not trying to be one of them. I can't be. I just want to learn about them. They discuss things I don't know, like philosophy and politics. They make references to books I never heard of. They make jokes I don't get. And most importantly, they are all taking Latin and in the Latin Club. I think the only people they respect are others in the Latin Club.

I beg my mother to let me take Latin next year.

"Mom, I can take one elective course next year. I want to take Latin."

"Don't be silly. Why would you take Latin?"

Of course, I can't confess to wanting to be something I am not. I can't say I want to be in the Latin Club.

"They say Latin is a good foundation for understanding where our language comes from." I know that is true because I heard a guy in the Latin Club say so.

"So? How is that useful?"

"Well," I say, my confidence waning, "it would make me smarter. I would be a better reader, and I would write better."

"It seems like you read just fine now. You read all the time! Why don't you take typing? That makes a lot more sense."

Not one girl in the Latin Club takes typing. Not one.

"I don't want to take typing. How is *typing* useful?" I ask, mimicking my mother's tone of voice.

"Don't be a smart aleck. Typing is very useful. You will always have that skill to fall back on."

I grimace. "Fall back on? From where am I falling?"

"Sign up for typing."

8

rolling

1956
age 15

THE ROLLER SKATER girls gather in the women's restroom to smoke cigarettes. I spend a lot of time pretending I have to go to the bathroom just so I can look at them and listen to them talk.

I have done this at least three times tonight.

I roll on my cheap rental skates into the restroom and glide through the middle of the girls in the lounge area. They ignore my existence. I roll on into the toilet area and into a stall. I can see and hear them through the skinny space where the door doesn't quite meet the edge of the stall. They sprawl around the lounge area of the restroom in their flashy skates and sparkly skating outfits. Most of them have bee-hive hairdos, and they all wear over-the-top makeup. I so admire them. They are brassy and bold. Their conversation is filled with "I told him to go screw himself" or "Did you try that purple eye shadow?" or "Whaddaya mean buy it, I lifted it from the 5&10!"

It's almost time to go home, so this is my last restroom sortie. As usual, after rolling into the toilet stall, I pull down my pants and bend over in a half squat in order to pee. My mother has drummed into me and my sisters to never, ever, sit down on a public toilet seat. Unfortunately, this time, the lock on the stall door doesn't work. Just as I am about to stand up, I instead roll right out of the stall, in crouch position, into the lounge area. I come to a stop in the middle of the bad girls, still bent over with my rear end exposed and my pants around my ankles. All talking ceases.

Then the room is filled with laughter . . . at me.

Time to die.

9

no hope for the hopeless

1961
age 20

LYING IS MY only way out of New Jersey and into the world. My parents expect me to go to the local teacher's college. I lie and tell them, and my minister, that I want to be a missionary. They agree that I can go to a church college five states away.

I arrive at the small college in the small college town in Michigan expecting a hotbed of sophistication and learning. Instead, it's high school with talk of boys and gossip.

My dormmates are here to get their Mrs. Degree. No discussions of literature, or art, or God, or of anything. I go to chapel early morning, every morning, as required.

I go to classes, I do the assignments, but something is amiss. I zipped through high school. I never needed to study. Everything taught already resided in my brain. I was born with a certain amount of knowledge and have used it up. But in college all the material is foreign. I can't learn. I am incapable of learning. I am dumb.

I begin cutting classes, staying up late, and sleeping in, and every quarter my grades go down. My parents ask why. I say I don't know. I am lying to everyone. If this continues, I will flunk out. I am the first person in my family to go to college, and I can't cut it. I am horrified that everyone will know I am dumb. I would rather people believe I got caught up in college life and didn't study. I would rather have my parents be disappointed in me because I didn't work at it than have them and everyone else know I cannot learn.

I am stuck between failure and failure.

I write to my parents. I don't know where else to go for comfort. I can't tell them I want out, that I cannot succeed in college. I pour my heart out and reveal the dreams of greatness I have been holding secret for most of my life. I am a trapped spirit.

"Mom and Dad, I am frustrated. I want to do something in this world. I want to travel everywhere. I want to help people; I want to do important things. I don't know what they are, but I know I do not want to just get married and have children."

My father writes in response. I am startled because he has never written before and is very self-conscious about his writing.

"Dear Jean: Your mother is sitting next to me, and this letter is from both of us. We love you very much, and we understand your desire to do something in the world. We are proud of you. Please understand that doing something in this world will happen for you when you have children. You will be the leader for your children."

I can't. I just cannot accept that this is my fate, this is my future.

How stupidly circular it is! If my only purpose is to raise children, and their purpose is to raise children, who is it that will change the world? And why can't it be me?

Because I am dumb. I am lost and alone.

I'm going home.

CONFORMITY

10

the day before the wedding

1962
age 21

"MOM, WHAT DOES it feel like to be in love?"

"You don't know?"

"I don't think so. How would I know if I knew?"

"Jean, what is wrong with you? When you are in love, you just know it. You really don't know? You don't feel it?"

"I don't think so."

"But you are getting married tomorrow. Do you want to get married?"

I am not quite yet twenty-one. I don't know anything about what I want.

I glance at my mother. She is looking down at her hands, folding and unfolding them and slowly shaking her head. I don't know what to say.

"Yes, I want to get married."

I can't tell my mother I am unsure I'm doing the right thing to get married. My doubts would be shocking to her.

I also can't tell her I am apprehensive about sex with my husband, more so given my childhood experience. Sex education from my mother was limited to prohibiting the use of tampons: "You should not use tampons. There is something inside of you that breaks when you have sex with your husband for the first time. A tampon might break it by mistake, then you wouldn't be a virgin anymore."

There's no reason not to marry my fiancé. I like him. He is a good-looking Michigander with blond hair and blue eyes. We met in the college Chapel Choir—him a baritone, me an alto.

He is thoughtful and kind. He says he loves me.

He asked me to marry him. I said yes, but knew I didn't feel the way I was supposed to feel when accepting a proposal. I think I was just happy to have another possible path open to me when I was about to drop out of college. It was perfectly acceptable to quit college because you were going to get married. No one had to know I flunked out.

I now work in an airplane factory, typing orders for air-plane parts. I am sad most of the time, although I smile as much as possible so that others don't know. My choices are to get married or type airplane parts orders forever.

I look at my mother sitting in the TV room they gave up for me to live in until I got married. I see tears forming in her eyes. I know she won't allow them to fall.

She clears her throat and says, "If you don't know whether you are in love, maybe you should reconsider get-ting married."

The future in-laws have arrived from Michigan, the dress is hanging in the closet, the church hall and photographer are booked. How could I reconsider? What would I say?

I can't reconsider. We will get married.

the wedding night

I RETREAT TO the bathroom to change into my beautiful peignoir set. In my family, you not only need to have a wedding gown; a matching nightgown and peignoir are also required. The set has to be pure white and flowing. It is the outward sign of virginity.

I love my peignoir set. It's a sign of sophistication and worldliness. It is what women wear on television or in the movies for intimate occasions. Just wearing it makes me less like myself and more like a sophisticated woman who is not nervous about sex.

I am nervous. No, I am afraid. I don't want to be touched. Being touched or touching brings bad memories, but I know this is part of marriage. My husband is a virgin, too, and I can tell he is nervous. We lie in the bed for a while just talking. Little by little, he begins touching me. He is sweet and gentle, he apologizes if anything offends me. He moves slowly. I am grateful for that. This activity is nothing like I have ever experienced. No one has ever touched my breasts or had their hands all over my body.

Then something entirely unexpected happens. My husband's hand makes contact with the right spot on my body. I experience that thing I hadn't known about, have never experienced. The word *orgasm* joins my vocabulary and my life. It isn't earth-shaking, but it is explosive and unlike anything I've ever felt. I like it and want more of it.

the day after the wedding

1962
age 21

"I HAVE TO talk fast. We're still at the motel. My husband went to get coffee."

"Are you OK? What's the matter?" asks my older and married sister.

"I have a problem."

"What?" She sounds alarmed.

"I slept last night with my husband." I don't know how else to bring up the topic.

"How was it?"

"It was OK." I rush on, "He . . . um . . . finished."

"OK, and—?"

"Yes, and, well, the stuff all ran out of me."

"What?"

"You know, the stuff. The stuff that came out of him."

"OK." She pauses. "So, what is the problem?"

"I said, it ran out of me."

"I am missing something. Did you not want it to?"

"We are trying to get pregnant right away so he doesn't have to go into the army. Isn't the stuff supposed to stay in me? I thought it was absorbed by my body and that's how I would get pregnant. I stayed in bed for a long time after we were done, with my butt against the wall and my legs straight up to keep it in, but it didn't work."

My sister is quiet. When she speaks, her voice is soft.

"No, it doesn't stay inside of you. There is nothing wrong with you. You don't need it to stay inside in order to get pregnant."

I am embarrassed by my ignorance and horrified that this sex thing involved stuff running out of me. I'm not sure it is worth that.

honeymoon

1962
age 21

I HAD HOPED for the Jersey Shore. Our honeymoon, however, is on a pig farm in Virginia. My thrifty husband's uncle owns the farm. There is a lovely hunting lodge. Two bedrooms, soaring ceilings, giant stone fireplace. But it is still a pig farm. My husband thought that, with its big hunting lodge, the farm would be great.

There are no people here, only pigs and a few cows. There is no TV, or restaurants, or movies, or anything. Just him, me, and the pigs. The pigs are not conversationalists.

A noise wakes me this morning, the second morning of our marriage. My husband is not beside me in the bed. A note is on his pillow: "Gone dove hunting. Be back whenever."

Company arrives; an enormous cow has stuck its head through the bedroom window. It opens its giant mouth and moos at me.

a new york city dinner

1962
age 21

MY HUSBAND PROMISED that after our honeymoon, we would go to New York City to visit his cousin and her husband, or, as he called them, his "strange" cousins. Both are actors. I am excited and intimidated. I cannot imagine talking to actors. Real actors.

His cousins live in Greenwich Village. I have never been to this part of the city. The buildings are only about five stories and trees line the sidewalk. Their gray, skinny city trunks look unhealthy, but the branches are alive with green buds. A bare-chested man sits on a window ledge several stories up, waving, like he is blessing us mortals down here on the street. The sidewalk is filled with people, although their pace is slower, more relaxed than uptown. Spanish music is coming from somewhere, a mournful ballad. A family is sprawled on the steps of his cousin's building, catching the breeze of this beautiful spring night. We step around them into the building and take a creaky elevator to the fourth floor.

I knock on the apartment door. It opens and I am blasted by sound and color. Jazz emanates from an unseen speaker. Paintings cover the walls, all the way to the ceiling. Some are just swirls of color, some are landscapes. I have never been in an apartment, never mind one in Greenwich Village. My eyes can't stay still, flying from a tiny, gold-framed portrait of an old woman from another century to a life-sized nude that just might be our host.

My husband talks with his cousin about family as we enter. I just stare, rendered mute by the careless, exotic beauty of my surroundings.

Books are crammed on shelves and strewn around the room on every available surface. Towers of them, about to topple over, are on the floor. There is a soft, cushy, over-stuffed couch with yellow, orange, and green African print pillows. I want to scrunch up among those pillows with a book.

Dinner turns out to be a dinner *party*. The table is set with beautifully mismatched dishes and old, silver candles. There are wine bottles on the table. Wine! With dinner!

The guests talk about a play they saw last weekend. They talk about literature, and politics, and spirituality, and acting. I don't know what food I'm eating, but it all tastes exotic and delicious. I want their lives. I want never to leave.

"And where are you from?" someone asks me.

"New Jersey" I respond, startled out of my invisibility. "A place everyone would like to be away from, I think."

Laughter erupts around the table. I should be given an Academy Award right then for overcoming my fright at being seen and heard by these magical people. And for making them laugh.

I look across the table at my husband. I am flying in an alternate universe and he doesn't notice. He is steadily eating his way through dinner, not part of the zinging energies.

We are not well-matched. I am not the same person I had been even just an hour before. I know right now this marriage probably will not work. I am sad and elated. I am frightened yet excited. I already am ashamed that I am going to abandon this good man at some point. I am not going to be the suburban housewife. I cannot be what was written for me.

15

labor

I CAN'T SEE my feet. My belly is in the way. A baby is going to be born anytime now. She is going to come out of my body. My mother tells me there will be pain, but as soon as the baby is born I will forget about the pain.

I don't believe it.

It is barely June in Fort Chaffee, Arkansas, but it is 104 degrees. My clothes rub against the heat rash spreading over my swollen body. There are cramps in my groin when I walk, and heartburn is my constant companion. The doctor says all this is normal. Nothing about this is normal. I complain to my husband, but what does he know? He is new at this too.

My mother calls from New Jersey.

"How is everything?"

"It's OK," I say, but it isn't. I'm not OK. I'm scared.

"You want me to come there? I can get a plane tomorrow and be there."

"No, I'm OK. Really."

I'm lying because this is something I want to do by myself, without her direction. I have something to prove here about being a real woman and a grown-up. Real women and grown-ups have babies all the time.

I wish I could stop thinking about what is going to happen, and how painful it will be, and whether I will survive. I worry all day, every day, about having the baby. I've been married fourteen months, I am nine months pregnant, and I am frightened beyond words.

My doctor is an army doctor. Why would anyone be a career army doctor when he can make so much more money on the outside? I've been seeing him every week, but he always is in a hurry and on his way somewhere else. I don't know how good he is, and I don't want to talk to him about being afraid. I think he would just laugh and be gone.

The pains start with mild twinges about eight in the evening. We are at a friend's house for dinner and watching TV. Indigestion has been my companion for so long I don't realize it is labor.

About ten o'clock, the pains start getting stronger, and I know.

My husband and the husband of our friend are watching TV, heavily engrossed in the movie "The Desert Fox."

The wife and I start calculating the time between my contractions. It's about seven or eight minutes. What I mostly feel is downward pressure, like the baby is straining to pop out all by itself. To me, that seems like an emergency, but no one else is worried.

"Shouldn't we go to the hospital?"

"It's a little early," says the wife, "your pains are not very long or strong yet."

Well, she should know. She's had two kids. But it feels like an emergency to me. I am just twenty-one years old. Fear is rising.

"Can we go to the hospital?" I ask my husband.

"Hang on, the movie is almost over."

I may never forgive him for those words.

delivery

WE GET TO the hospital at about eleven in the evening. I see no doctors and begin to panic. My labor pains are six minutes apart.

"Where is my doctor?"

"No need to be upset," says the nurse, "when it is close to time, we will call him."

They hustle me into a labor room, away from my husband, my only support, the only person who cares about me.

"Can't my husband stay with me while I'm in labor?"

"No, husbands are not allowed in the labor room. We have to have privacy for all women in labor."

"Privacy? I'm the only one here. Why can't he be with me?"

"Someone might come in. Besides, it's against the rules."

I am alone in this room by myself for hours and hours. One small window, no books, no telephone, a tiny TV up on the wall. No one to hear me cry.

The nurses come by occasionally to time the pains and measure how much my cervix has dilated. They are very nice, but no one is here when the pain is so intense I think I cannot bear it. No one holds my hand through the hard parts. No one tells me it will all be OK. No one gives me a hug. I can't stop the tears. I wish my mother were here.

It's almost morning. I see the sky lighten through the little window. The labor pains are more intense and closer together. The doctor arrives, laughing and joking with the nurses. I don't know what is funny. He looks at me, feels my stomach, and measures how far I am dilated, but he doesn't seem to see me. He is involved in routine, while I am involved in terror.

The labor pains are more than I can stand. I thought they would give me something for pain, but they said no. I don't know why. It seems I am hardly through one awful cramping pain when another begins. The doctor god decides it is time to deliver the baby. They roll me into the delivery room, and they must have given me something because everything goes blurry. The pain is less, and I am floating somewhere above the bed. I can hear every word spoken but can't seem to speak.

"Huh, the baby is a face-forward birth," says the doctor.

"Doctor, do you mean it is a breech birth?"

"No. Not unless it has eyes, nose, and mouth on its ass."

I am no longer cognizant of anything. I am somewhere else. I wake up in a hospital bed in a new ward. Within minutes of coming awake, I remember. I just had a baby whose eyes, nose, and mouth are on her ass. What will we do? Can the baby live? I can't stand this. I am just a baby myself. How can I deal with this?

A nurse comes in.

"Where is my husband?"

"He went home to sleep. He was here all night and was very worried about you and the baby. He'll be back soon. Do you want to see the baby?"

What? See the baby? See the monster?

"I can see her?"

"Sure, why not?"

"Because the doctor said she wasn't born right."

I can't say the words he used. The nurse seems unconcerned, like disaster is not on the horizon.

"Oh no, hon. I was there. Usually, babies come out top-of-head first. Your baby was born face-first. That's all. Probably means she is going to be a go-getter in this world! She is fine. The doctor was just joking with us."

I am not laughing.

"OK."

She comes in with the baby and plops her in my arms. I look down. There is a face. A tiny, perfect, almost smiling face. I am relieved.

17

strange feelings

1963
age 22

I CALL MY mother from the hospital.

"I had to go back into the hospital because I have some
sort of infection. Can you come take care of the baby?"

"Of course! I will fly there tomorrow. Are you OK?"

"I think so. I should get out in a couple of days, but the
baby . . . I'm breastfeeding her. I don't know what to do about
that. How will she eat?"

I'm asking even though I know there are ways to deal with
interruptions to nursing. I am worried she won't remember

how to nurse when I get out. What I can't explain to my mother, or even to myself, is the strange new feeling that has claimed residence.

It is a kind of loneliness. A longing.

It feels like my baby is calling me home.

second coming

1966
age 25

I HEAD FOR the comfortable chair to put my feet up when *whoosh!* Some sort of fluid is running down my legs and pooling on the floor. This is not in the program. I do not know what is happening. My husband is in the Presbyterian seminary library studying for a theology exam. I don't want to call the library and tell them there is an emergency until I know whether there is. I call my sister the nurse.

"Oh help! Something has happened. I might be having a miscarriage."

"What do you mean a miscarriage? You are almost nine months pregnant. What happened?"

"I was just walking to the living room and yellowish water started pouring out of me!"

"Ah, your water broke."

"What?"

"Sometimes, labor starts this way rather than just with pains."

"I don't know about this. Nothing like this happened last time."

"Well, you have been pretty adamant about not learning about pregnancy."

"If it's natural, it should be natural. Why should I study it?"

"Um . . . because you are standing in a pool of fluid and don't know why."

"What should I do?"

"Clean it up and call your doctor. It's not an emergency, but you have to alert him."

My doctor says my labor pains should start soon and to contact them if they don't start within the next day or so.

It doesn't take a day. It doesn't even take an hour. The pains start hard and fast. I call the library and ask them to find my husband and send him home. We are at the hospital within the hour.

The labor and birth processes haven't changed much since my first baby. My husband still cannot be with me in the labor room. He says he will go and study in the waiting room. I really don't know why it would hurt for my husband to be with me at these momentous times.

In the delivery room, they give me something for pain, although it doesn't make me feel floaty like the last time. They have a mirror up above where the doctor sits on a stool at my feet.

It is there so I can watch the baby being born. I don't want to watch. The sight of my vagina, which I have never before seen, with a large head protruding from it, does me in. Thankfully, this baby is born fast. Compared to the last delivery, this is a breeze. The baby is plump, beautiful, and calm, seemingly at home immediately with her new surroundings.

They roll me out of the delivery room and stop at a wall phone just outside of it. The nurse dials the waiting room and asks to speak to my husband. The nurse hands the phone to me.

"Hello?" says my husband.

"Hi," I say.

"Who is this?" he asks.

questions, questions

1966
age 25

What am I doing here?
What do I want?
Am I limited forever?
Are there no choices?
Why do I want?
Why am I longing?

I've stopped dreaming.

STIRRING

20

say his name

1968
age 27

THE CHURCH JANITOR asks for time off to attend Martin Luther King Jr.'s funeral. The senior pastor asks why he would go to the funeral. The janitor reveals that Coretta Scott King is his niece.

The elders and deacons at the church are horrified at this revelation. A hastily called meeting is held. There are accusations that the janitor had "insinuated himself into our midst" by being employed as the church janitor . . . for over forty years. There are calls to fire him.

ALFRED LLOYD TENNYSON SCOTT

None of what I hear about this meeting fits into the picture presented to us when we moved to Alabama just three months ago. On that rainy January day, we were greeted by church members who gifted us with a clutch of deep red camellia blossoms. I was grateful and thought maybe my impressions of Alabama were not correct. The church people warmly welcomed their new assistant pastor and family. "So glad your sweet family is here." Gracious and loving people.

On our first day at the church, we met the staff, including the janitor. He is the only black person on the staff, probably in his 60s, and is introduced only as Alfred. My husband asked for his last name, and from then on, my husband and I address him as Mr. Scott.

My husband asked the senior pastor, "Do Mr. Scott and his family attend church here?"

"Alfred is here to open the church on Sundays, then close it when the service is over. He and his family would be welcome to attend services, but he prefers not to. We installed a sound system in the church hall. We thought Alfred would be more comfortable listening to the service from there."

I don't know what is true and not true, but I have my doubts about what I just heard.

They must have paid hundreds of dollars to put a public address system into the church hall. I don't have the nerve to ask the pastor any questions. I tuck this information away to think about later.

Later seems to be now at this meeting to address Mr. Scott's deviousness and his "communist" connections with the King family. The rhetoric gets uglier. "There is a viper in our midst." "We can't have him here. Who knows what he will do. Look how he hid his connection to King."

For forty years, the church members had only referred to Mr. Scott as Alfred. They didn't know or care about his last name. And now, according to them, this was a trick he played on them. They believe that for all those years he hid his identity from them on purpose. Only strong words from the senior pastor prevent his firing.

Mr. Scott is granted the time off by the senior pastor and goes to the funeral. The next Sunday, Mr. Scott is at his usual post at the church.

21

awakening

1972
age 31

I WANT NO part of the church. I have no taste for the bla-
tantly racist betrayal of the black janitor employed for forty
years. I go to church less and less. My husband says people
are talking about me, that I'm not being a good minister's
wife. I don't care what they think or say. My husband keeps
trying to work with church members, but with no changes of
hearts or minds. I want to leave the church. For the first time,
I make my thoughts known to my husband when I disagree
with him. Finally, he, too, is done with it, and we leave the
church entirely.

My husband joins the army as a Chaplain. He is ordered to South Korea. The girls and I will stay in Mobile.

My husband leaving for a year angers and frightens me. I had accepted my assigned fate as wife, mother, and helper as best I could. And now the mainstay of the family, the head of the family, is going away?

"You are leaving me on my own to take care of everything? You just go because you want to go?"

It is a betrayal of the contract we had, the arrangement I agreed to.

I worry I won't be able to cope without him, but really what I am afraid of is that he will change and grow away from me. He will see the world. He will have adventures. He will grow. Then he will come home to boring me.

"You will do just fine. Both of the girls will be in school. Why don't you take some classes at the university since you are here anyway with nothing to do? It will keep you busy."

He may as well have patted me on the head.

emerging

1972
age 31

I GO BACK to college. I talk myself into it; I hadn't done well the last time. I have to make this time different. The University of South Alabama offers a remedial course on how to study, so I take it. I am thirty-one years old, sitting in a classroom with eighteen-year-old kids to learn how to study, but I am not embarrassed to be so much older. I am here to do this thing.

Surprise. Learning is just a process.

I am not dumb. I just didn't know how to learn, how to study. I may even be smart. The world beyond what I know becomes less mysterious and more within my reach. I begin getting great grades and, even more importantly, I begin to love learning. I am hungry for it. I feel as if the top of my head has opened and sunshine is streaming in. I wake every morning in happy anticipation of the day. Life is exciting, and I am filled with a passion for living it.

Some university students are involved in the anti-war movement and the civil rights movement. I first watch them, admiring their passion and fire, then I start hanging out with these young men and women. They are so alive and they have such strong feelings of purpose. Before long, my girls and I are at civil rights marches, demonstrations, concerts, and sit-ins. I sit on the ground at yet another demonstration, a daughter on each side of me.

"Are you having a good time?"

"Yes," yells my older daughter, "this is fun!"

Our lives become rounds of crowd events. I love it. There is a presidential election on the horizon, and I jump on the McGovern-for-president bandwagon. I co-create an underground "revolutionary" newspaper that undermines and exposes the local white power structure. Life is filled with color and grand gestures and high feelings of power and possibility. I am thriving and my daughters are thriving. Life is nonstop adventure.

But then my husband preaches an anti-war sermon on the army base in Korea. The military is not about to put up with that. They give him a choice: resign your commission or be court-martialed. He resigns his commission and comes home, with very little notice.

trouble

MY HUSBAND'S UNEXPECTED homecoming from Korea shocks both of us. He is not happy with how I have changed while he was gone. And how can I blame him? He did nothing wrong. I just tasted freedom. He wants his wife back.

I subdue my passions. I stop the myriad anti-war and civil rights activities to return the family to some semblance of what used to be. I go to school, my husband looks for work, we eat dinner together. We get babysitters and go out visiting as we used to. Our nine-year-old daughter begins acting out, stealing money from our wallets to buy french fries and cokes for the neighborhood kids. She is angry at her father, but angrier at me. She throws all her dolls into the trash. "I am not a child. I don't NEED a babysitter."

I elevated my children to companion status while my husband was gone, then abruptly sent them back to childhood. I think I have done the same thing to myself.

choice

1973
age 32

Two children, long agreed,
Playing at our feet as we talk through the choices.

I fly alone to where it is legal.
The nurse holds my hand through it all.

Nascent is no more.

I cry. I claim my choice.
I cry. Not in regret.

I cry.

falling apart

1974
age 33

MY HUSBAND AND I barely speak now. He tries to understand the new me, but it is too difficult for him. He wants
me home to cook dinner and take care of our girls. He
wants me to continue the role I signed up for.

I can't meet his expectations, but when I do, I meet them
grudgingly. I don't want to take up that role again. I get a
job selling radio advertising. I can justify it because he is
still looking for work. The job keeps me on the road around
Mobile all day every day. And after work, I go out for drinks

with friends. I don't want to go home. Our neighbor, struck by my frequent absences and the close care my husband gives to our children, asks him whether I am their real mother.

My husband suggests marital counseling. I agree. I want our marriage to survive. I want a whole family for our children, but I want it to be different than before. We go to a local pastor. It is quickly clear that these are "fix Jean" sessions. Jean is not interested anymore in having sex with her husband? Fix Jean. Give the couple gentle sex exercises to do together. Jean is spending too much time outside of the family? Fix Jean. Create conversation about the sacredness of family.

I am at a breaking point. I am torn into pieces. What am I doing? Who am I hurting? How can I go back? How can I go forward? Back is suffocation. Back is giving up. Back is a dullness in my brain. Back is not tolerable.

Forward is destruction of my family.

26

———

telling the parents

———

1974
age 33

"I AM GETTING divorced."

I have dropped a bomb on Thanksgiving. My sister herds the kids downstairs to clear the decks.

My mother and father look stunned. I can tell the words make no sense to them. I have been married for twelve years and have two children. I have never told my parents I am unhappy in my marriage.

"What are you talking about?" asks my mother. "You can't just get divorced!"

"I have filed for divorce."

"How can you do this? You have children! You can't break up your family. That is a terrible thing!" My mother's face is flushed with outrage.

I don't respond. Mom's voice raises.

"Does he drink? Does he mistreat you? He is a minister for goodness' sake, and you have children. What are you thinking? Why would you say such a thing?"

I focus on her use of "say such a thing."

"I can't believe you. If you had a good reason, I might understand it. What is your reason?"

I could never explain my unhappiness to my mother. She would not understand or approve of my reasons. I remain silent. I have been dreading this moment.

"Well, why?" Mom is yelling.

"I'm not going to tell you. My reasons are my reasons."

With those words, I commit the cardinal family sin. I say something I know will upset my mother but say it anyway.

Mom's voice keeps rising. "You're not going to tell us? You are going to do something so awful, and you're not going to say why?"

I turn to my father, feeling my resolve to keep my reasons to myself slipping away with every shot from my mother. My father doesn't speak, the role he plays in every family fuss. I know he doesn't want to make Mom even more upset, which he certainly would if he spoke up for me.

"You simply cannot destroy a family for no good reason," yells my mother. "You cannot!" She begins to cry, turns away, and heads for a bedroom. Even worse than Mom upset is Mom crying.

My resolve breaks. I get up to go to my mother and try to justify why I am divorcing my husband.

My father speaks. "Stop," he says. "Don't go in there."

"I have to. Mom is so upset. She's crying!"

"No need. It's OK."

"But Dad, Mom is crying. . . ."

"Leave your mother alone. She will get over this, she will be OK. You do what you need to do."

I didn't know I had that choice.

PREPARING

i am woman

1974
age 33

"SO, DO YOU think women should wear the pants in the family? I like to see legs."

"Isn't it dumb to say women should earn the same as men when men have families to support?"

"Do you know the Bible says men are to be the head of the household?"

The obnoxious questions come thick and fast. I am the speaker for a newly formed women's rights group. Invitations to speak occur more often as word of our group gets out, yet the invitations are to men's organizations, like the Rotary Club or Kiwanis. We do not get invitations to speak to women's civic organizations, like the Junior League.

My speeches are serious, historical, and academic, intended to educate and persuade. I steal parts of speeches from national figures because I don't know how to say what I want to say, or quite what I want to talk about. We newborn feminists are still trying to understand ourselves, and women who are different from ourselves, and to struggle with new concepts about interactions between men and women. How could we not have thought before about what it is to be female? Not noticed that we are, at best, second-class citizens?

It is clear in the Q&A sessions after my speeches that the invitations to speak are for entertainment rather than enlightenment: I am comic relief so the men can laugh at me and the whole women's movement. I am openly mocked. I am a "women's libber," and once that descriptor is attached to me, all the much-ballyhooed southern gentleman stuff goes out the window.

I accept the men's invitations for my own purposes. I know I'm never going to convince these good old boys of anything. These club meetings, however, are always reported in the local newspaper. "The Rotary Club hosted Mrs. Jean Peelen to speak this month. Mrs. Peelen is the founder of a new women's lib organization in Mobile."

It is my hope that women seeing these articles may want to reach out to us for support.

Despite my intention to remain poised and calm during Q&A, it is not easy to keep my temper in check in the face of mocking disrespect and open hostility.

"You want a female cop to show up at the bank robbery?" asks one Kiwanis genius.

"Are you a Lesbian?" sneers another balding, overweight member.

"Are you my alternative?" I snap back.

Laughter rounds the room. My eyes open to the magic of humor leveling the playing field.

I am woman.

gloria and flo

GLORIA STEINEM AND Florynce Kennedy are coming to speak! I am beyond excited. My heroes of the women's movement will be right here at The University of South Alabama.

We bitty band of feminists don't know how the speaking invitation happened, but are beside ourselves with joy. Our icons are coming! We will be able to see them, to hear them, to learn from them.

We offer to help with transport. "Let us take some of the burden of this event. We will pick up Ms. Steinem and Ms. Kennedy at the airport."

"Are you sure?"

"Oh yes, oh yes, oh yes."

We prepare ourselves for this momentous visit. I read everything Gloria or Flo has ever said or written so as not to embarrass myself with them. Friend Leila makes T-shirts for us to wear to the airport and to give to Gloria and Flo as welcome presents. They are amazing shirts. Across the top, in glittery letters is written "Southern Feminists." Below the words is a drawing of a giant, colorful, over-frosted cupcake (oh those sweet, southern women). An evil-looking razor-blade is sticking up from the frosting.

Three of us stand at the airport arrival gate, in our Southern Feminist T-shirts, waiting for our heroes to come off the plane. "There she is! There's Flo!" "Where is Gloria?" "Here she comes!"

The legends come through the gate scanning the crowd for their escorts. They look unlike any other people at the airport. Both are impressively tall, and their strides brook no interference. Gloria is elegant, in skinny jeans and impressive New York boots. Flo is a movie version of a western cowhand: boots, leather vest, and wide-brimmed cowboy hat. Flo's eyes stop on us. She hoots with laughter. "Look! Look at them! They have to be our escorts." Flo and Gloria grab us and hug us. They cannot stop laughing at our shirts.

"Are you all from Alabama?" asks Gloria.

"They are," I say. "I'm just an honorary Southerner."

"Just a minute," says Leila in her soft southern voice. "We have something for you."

She pulls two more T-shirts out of her bag and gives one to Gloria and one to Flo.

"Oh no!" Gloria says.

I think, oh dear, they won't wear them. How could we have thought they would? How embarrassing.

Both women drop their carry-on bags and pull the T-shirts over their heads.

"Let's go," says Flo.

The five of us stride out of the airport arm in arm. Game on.

knitting in law school

1975
age 34

KNIT ONE, PURL one. Knit one, purl one.

I sit and I knit in almost all my law school classes.

Every class is lecture, with no discussion. Questions are designed only to determine whether the reading assignment has been completed. I don't concern myself about these little torture rituals since it is unlikely I or the few other women in my classes will be called on. We are invisible to the majority of professors.

All but one law professor is male.

MADAME DeFARGE

In the entering class before mine, there were only two women. In my class, twenty-five percent of us are female. It wasn't easy to get here, and I am petrified I could fail at all of it.

Knit one, purl one.

By the end of the winter, I will have outfitted my children and several of my classmates with scarves and mittens.

During most classes, my head is bowed over my knitting. When I do occasionally look up, I look unsmiling at the professors. My Criminal Law professor complains to the Dean that I stare at him with menace while knitting during his class. The Dean thinks it important to investigate this allegation of improper staring.

"Why are you staring in a hostile manner at the professor in class? It makes everyone uncomfortable."

"Because he told a bad joke."

"What kind of bad joke?"

"A racist and sexist bad joke about the price of prostitutes."

"Which was?"

"I will not repeat it."

The investigation is dropped.

Not to be outmaneuvered, the professor calls several male students from the Criminal Law class into his office to express his concerns about me. In law school, the identity of final exam takers is not known to the professors. Intimidation is their only weapon.

"I am troubled about our class," says the professor.

"Why?" They ask.

"One student is being so disruptive to the class and disrespectful to me."

"Who?"

"The knitter. It's upsetting that she doesn't really participate in the class. She looks like she is always judging me. The distress she causes could affect my grades for the whole class."

Instead of the students going directly to the Dean to report this extortion attempt, one of the group members comes to talk to me. There he stands, white, male, and privileged.

"We had a meeting with the professor. He says your attitude could affect the grades for the whole class. I know you are a very nice person. Please stop knitting and smile more. Can't you see how your behavior could affect us all?"

"I know you, too, are a very nice person. Now fuck off."

competing interests

1976
age 35

I sit between my lover and his mother,
His nerves in rapid speech
Her face unbroken by smiles.

I am eleven years older than he,
And eleven years younger than she.
I have more in common with her.

I am divorced with two children and done.
He is single and not had one.
Mama is watching her dreams disappear.

My sympathy is for his mom.
My lust is for her son,
My first taste of passion.

anything is possible

1976
age 35

THE PHONE RINGS in the middle of the day. An unusual thing in our house since everyone knows I'm normally in law class in the afternoons.

"Hello?"

"Hi honey, it's Mom."

"Are you OK? Is Dad OK?"

"Your dad and I are fine, but I have some bad news. Uncle Roy died."

My heart picks up its beat again. Parents are OK. Uncle Roy isn't, but I have never liked Uncle Roy.

We all love our Aunt Ruthie. She is so loving and giving. But she always seems anxious and apologetic around him. He is, or was, so grudging and crabby. He rarely spoke, and when he did it was more like barking short sentences. "Gotta go pen the goats." "Don't like the damn peas."

Since we were little kids, my mother had told us to stay away from Uncle Roy. She did not say why. I didn't want to be around him anyway and did as I was told but was curious about why my mother wouldn't say.

We would only visit Uncle Roy and Aunt Ruthie once or twice a year because they lived two hours away. When we were there, Uncle Roy mostly stayed out in the barn. He would come in for dinner and then join the rest of us in the living room afterward. The parents all took the big overstuffed comfy chairs. My sister and I, and our boy cousin, would play some board or card game on the floor. My girl cousin, my age, always sat on her father's lap. I wondered what she liked about him. I loved my father, too, but I didn't sit on his lap.

Even though it was no hardship to stay away from Uncle Roy, I kept pushing my mother on the "why" of it. It was rare that my mother was mysterious. The most she ever offered was "I didn't like the way he acted with me when I was little."

I knew there was more. There had to be more. Mom clamped her jaw and offered no more information.

"*Oh nooooo,*" I say sympathetically about Uncle Roy's death, knowing as I say it that I'm not at all dismayed by the news. "I'm sorry to hear he died." I'm not really sorry but am adhering to my mother's cardinal rule to never speak ill of family. "What did he die of?"

There is silence on Mother's end.

"Mom? How did he die?"

"Well, he hung himself in the barn."

"Oh my god. He did? He really did? He committed suicide?"

"Oh no. None of us would ever do that. Our family doesn't do that."

"Then—what?"

"Well, you know Uncle Roy was old. And when we get older, we start getting shorter. We think Uncle Roy didn't like how much he had shrunk. We think he was just trying to stretch his neck."

an ill wind

1977
age 36

TORNADO WARNINGS ARE blasting from the TV. The sky is a green I've never seen. It appears all of nature has stopped moving, stopped breathing, and is waiting. My younger daughter is in the bathtub, cushioned by myriad pillows, clutching a cat under each arm. The older daughter is making fun of her.

"Scaredy cat!"

We hear shouting. I race outside. A police car is cruising by. An officer with a bullhorn is leaning out the passenger side window. "Take shelter! Take shelter! The tornado is at the Kmart!"

I just stand here, gawking and disbelieving what I hear. I have an overwhelming desire to laugh, yet my logical mind wants to compute: "Let's see. The Kmart is about five miles away. How fast does a tornado move again?"

"Go to your designated shelter! Now!"

The Alabama National Guard Armory shelter is about a mile away. OK. Maybe we should go. Maybe we should go right now. I force my daughters to leave our cats behind. We jump in our car and race to the Armory. The place is huge. I see a large group of adults and children standing on the porch of the main entrance.

We park and run to the entrance. Everyone standing on the porch is black. Whole families are huddled together. Children are clinging to parents. I also see white uniformed military personnel standing inside in front of the doors.

"What's going on?" I ask.

"They won't let us in."

"What? This is the shelter. What do you mean?"

The door guards inside are stone-faced. I don't know whether they can hear us, but they surely can see us.

"The doors are locked."

"What?"

This makes no sense. Are we at the wrong place?

I rattle the doors, then start banging on them. The guards inside do not move, do not speak, do not acknowledge our existence. I yell at them to open the damn doors. I wonder why someone in the crowd hasn't already done these things.

I keep banging and yelling. One of the guards speaks into a walkie-talkie.

Within a few minutes, some new guy shows up inside and gives a command. The doors are unlocked. We are ushered in and directly into a little room. One whole side of the room is windows. The military guys now are stationed at the door of the room we are in.

I am disgusted and angry. I know being let in the building is the direct result of a white person showing up at the front door. I know that. I *know* that. A white person demanding that the doors be opened is what opened the doors. I also am clear that the guards at the door of this little room are to keep the black people inside of it. I go to the guard and demand to see the commander in charge.

They take me to him. Of course they do.

"How dare you!" I say. "How dare you keep us waiting outside when there is a tornado coming. These are your neighbors! They were frightened. The children were crying.

Why didn't you let them in? And why do you have us confined in that little room?"

"Calm down, Miss, it's not your business. But for your information, we would have let them in if we knew a tornado was headed directly for us."

"But not ahead of time? You wouldn't let them into our designated shelter ahead of the disaster?"

"No," he replied. "We can't have those people running the halls in here."

a chukker bar farewell

"WHAT THE HELL is that?"

I follow his gaze up to the ceiling at a mural of god hand-ing Adam a can of beer.

"We call it the Sistine Chukker."

"Is that supposed to be funny?"

"Oh, probably not."

I am losing interest in keeping him interested. The tint of his skin, the way the hair curls at the back of his neck tickles desire. But only tickles. I am leaving soon. I have a dream to chase. He has a career to climb, a wife to find, and children to create. "I wanted to meet you at a *real* bar that serves more than beer."

I look at him.

"You are moving to Washington, DC. Washington is *not* Tuscaloosa. You have to be more sophisticated. You can't be a beer drinker in DC."

"I didn't know that," I say as I sip my beer.

"Right. That's why I'm telling you."

He is obnoxious, but maybe he is right.

"You'll be dealing with other attorneys, high-level government officials, and civil rights groups. You can't just drink beer!"

"What should I drink?"

"Scotch."

"Ugh. Tried it once. Hated the taste."

"Everybody hates it the first time. You'll get used to it."

BLOOMING

cream of the crop

1978
age 37

FIVE OTHER NEWLY minted attorneys line this side of the table with me. Their average age is 24. Good god, I was having babies at 24. They are all spiffy: the men in their dark suits and red ties, the women in the feminized version, bows replacing ties. I look down at my flowered dress from Sears bought especially for the job.

The Assistant General Counsel for Civil Rights smiles from across the table. "Welcome to your first job. I expect you to be outstanding. You are the cream of the crop."

I barely made it into the top half of my graduating class. I co-authored one legal brief in my whole life. I am not dressed appropriately.

My lower leg and foot start shaking.

35

lemon meringue

1979
age 38

"HOW COULD HE leave without saying anything to anybody?"
asks Old Joe. He swivels unsteadily on his semi-permanent
home, third barstool from the left.

"I don't know."

"Well, you *should* know. You were his girlfriend and all."

I cringe a little at the title. It's true, I had liked him. He's
an artist. I had slept with him . . . a lot. He had to return
home sometime. But to just go? Without a word?

"Why did he leave?"

"I guess he has to teach. He was on sabbatical here." My voice is not steady.

"Did he tell you he was going?"

"You know he didn't."

The discussion is joined by fellow barflies.

"Well, I'm pissed at him," says one. "It's not right what he did."

Boozy heads nod all around.

"I'd like to tell him what for," says the bartender.

"I'd like to throw a pie in his face," says Old Joe, "and tell him it's from all of us!"

"Oh, that's crazy. He's in Colorado!"

"We'll take up a collection," says Hat Mary from the other end of the bar. "We'll fly Jean out to hit him with the pie."

"Let the punishment fit the crime!" bellows Joe, almost losing his seat on the stool.

Everyone starts pulling out their wallets. They are serious!

"I'll contribute if you bring back proof you hit him with the pie." says the bartender.

"OK. I'll go," I say.

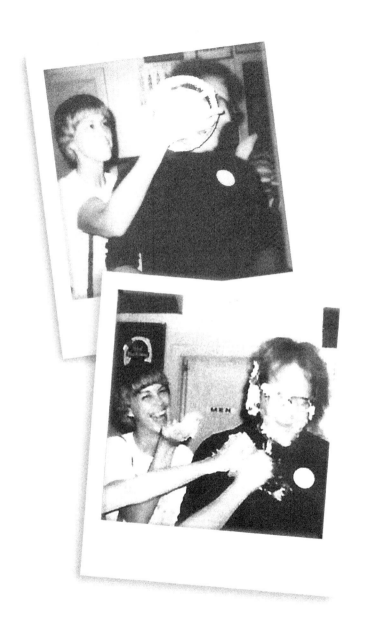

don't fence me out

I HAVE ONE leg over the top of the tall fencing when the searchlight hits me. The DC metro police car pulls further into the alley and stops. "Freeze!"

There is not a single excuse I can make for where I am and what I am doing.

The bar manager's parting words as he closed the bar tonight, "Sure, come on over to my place anytime" meant "come on over tonight." I didn't know about any security fence, but between me and Johnny Walker Red, I wasn't going to let that stop me.

I freeze as ordered, working to keep my balance on top of the fence. Oh god, I can picture the headline in the Washington Post: "Federal attorney arrested breaking into local bar manager's house."

I am hot for the bar manager. I look at him and see bad boy romance. He is everything I shouldn't want: a high school dropout, a Vietnam marine, a macho man, a bar manager. He is the direct opposite of what the world would have me look for: a successful lawyer or businessman.

But I see tall, tough, smart, funny, rule-breaker, and very, very sexy.

I hear laughter. The cops are *laughing*. "He must be *really* good at it," one snickers from within the car. I know the voice. It is one of the many cops that hang out at his bar. They know him and they know me.

The bar manager's back door opens. He comes out, baseball bat held as weapon. "What the hell?" he says.

"Oh, it's just one of your friends come to see ya!" yells the cop.

The bar manager grabs my hand to help me over.

"Welcome," he says.

beers with clarence t.

THE WAREHOUSE BAR is filling up with softball players. My boss, Clarence Thomas, Assistant Secretary for Civil Rights, is already ensconced at our table with his beer. The beer and the conversations are flowing, but, as is his way, Clarence is the quietest person here. I'm not sure why he comes to our softball games and goes with us to drink afterward. I think he is lonely. His wife isn't with him. Word is they are separated.

We all try to chat with him, as one does with the big boss, to make him more comfortable, or to find some common

ground, or to impress him. I'm always trying to figure him out. It's hard for me to talk with introverts, and Clarence is that: introverted and socially awkward.

I listen in on a conversation when the shortstop asks Clarence about his family. "Four brothers and one sister," he says.

The chatter goes on about his siblings, mostly about his brothers.

I see my opportunity to participate. "What about your sister? Is she still in Georgia? What is she like?"

"Yes, she still is there. She has kids and is on welfare."

"Oh, that's hard," I say.

"Do you help her out?" asks the left-fielder.

"No. I don't approve of welfare. She has children. What kind of example does that set for her children?"

There is quiet around the table. No one wants to take on the boss.

The left-fielder, maybe unwisely, persists. "You don't financially help her at all? That isn't welfare, that is helping your sister and her children."

"No. She needs to learn to be self-sufficient, to support herself and her children."

Chills. I feel chills.

38

unsportsmanlike conduct

1984
age 43

THE WOMEN'S ATHLETICS Director signals me from her end of the huge conference table with a subtle eyebrow raise every time the Men's Athletics Director speaks. "Excuse me," I say to the assembled elite of this NCAA Big 10 University. "Is there a restroom near here?"

"I'll show her where it is," the Women's Athletics Director offers.

"What's up?" I ask as we enter the restroom, although I suspect I know. This is not my first rodeo.

"Those figures they just gave you about how much gets spent on recruiting male basketball players as compared to female basketball players are totally bogus."

"What is the truth?"

"They are hiding that the University started and supports a men's basketball booster club. The club raises tens of thousands each year for men's basketball, including recruitment costs. There is no women's basketball booster club and no effort to create one."

"Anything else I should know?"

"Yes. Your tour skipped the women's weight room. That's because there isn't one. There are some barbells in the locker room and that's it. You saw the men's, right?"

"Yes, state of the art."

"Thank you. I'd better get back," she says glancing nervously at the restroom door.

"Wait, one more thing. They said the female athletes have equal access to the trainers and physical therapists. Is that true?"

"Of course not. They only get to see a trainer or therapist if the men aren't using them."

I go back to the table. I want to speak up to the University President and the General Counsel. I want to say "Liar, liar, pants on fire."

I don't. I tuck this information away. It will be documented and end up in the final report.

recipe for dead cat in winter

———

1989
age 45

Ingredients:
One grown, crying daughter
One daughter's careless husband
One fourth floor apartment
One open window
One dead cat
One pizza restaurant freezer
One tiny coffin, with small window for viewing
One national park
One shovel

One boombox
Comforting music (e.g., "Over the Rainbow," preferably by
    Judy Garland)
One minister (or reasonable facsimile)
Frozen ground

Directions:
This recipe can only work if the husband who scared the cat
    out of the fourth floor window truly did it by mistake. If
    not a mistake, divorce husband immediately.
Place cat, well-wrapped, in freezer in friend's pizza restaurant
    to await spring burial. Do not tell restaurant employees.
When notified by restaurant that city inspectors are coming,
    retrieve frozen cat as quickly as possible.
Have carpenter friend build small, adorable coffin.
Take crying daughter, frozen cat, coffin, shovel, and boom
    box, to a national park. Place cat in coffin. If cat is
    frozen and won't fit into coffin, either wait for it to thaw
    or break its legs.
Once cat is thawed, fold legs gently into coffin. Dig hole
    in frozen ground. If that proves difficult, make crying
    daughter ask passers-by for help.
Play "Over the Rainbow" on the boombox. If minister fails
    to appear, pretend to be one and say appropriate words

*over dead cat. You should avoid words like "thrown,"
"window," and "stupid fool."*
Get daughter another cat ASAP.

special ed

I AM ON my usual post-speech high. There is a crowd around me after my speech at the national Children with Disabilities conference. I love representing the Office for Civil Rights at these conferences. I talk for a long time with special ed teachers, school principals, school superintendents, and attorneys for school districts, explaining again the legal requirement to provide an appropriate education to their students with disabilities.

The teachers simply want their students to succeed. The administrators are caught in the "we can't do this" paradigm. "We don't have the money. We don't have the staff."

The attorneys are trying to parse the law and gain my agreement that schools "really don't have to do that much" to comply with the law. The attorneys are misleading their clients, but I enjoy the verbal scuffles with them about the finer points of the law and regulations.

I see a group of three women hanging around the edge of the group. They are quiet. They don't shout questions or demand attention. They are just waiting to talk.

"What can I do for you?" I ask.

"We are mothers of kids with disabilities," one of them responds. "My daughter is in the first grade. She is categorized as visually impaired, but she has almost no vision at all. The school says they don't have anyone qualified to teach her and don't have the money to hire anyone to do so." Her voice raises. "We know she should go to a special school, but we don't have the money to send her there, and the school district refuses to pay for it."

She points to another mother. "Her son has a cognitive impairment. He is in the third grade getting no special help and is failing every subject." The third-grader's mother starts to speak but is overwhelmed by emotion and turns away, wiping her eyes.

The third mother joins in. "My child has ADHD-related behavior issues. The school says ADHD is not a recognized learning issue. They keep suspending him from school. This week they said my son is too disruptive to come to school. They told me to keep him home and they will send a tutor once a week."

"Can you help us?"

My self-importance balloon deflates. I have forgotten about the mothers and their children.

41

a rose tattoo

1991
age 50

I WANT A sweet little rose tattooed on my right breast. It's my fiftieth birthday. Got to do *something* special.

My mother and now-adult daughters are horrified. Probably just the result I am aiming for. A local dentist was recommended to me. Tattooing is a sideline for him. What could go wrong? I drive after-hours to his little dental office attached to his house in the Northern Virginia suburbs.

"Good," I think, "I don't have to go into one of those grungy tattoo parlors."

The dentist seems nice. Shows me a picture of a little rose. Looks perfect. He begins to work. Even though the little rose is to be located on my breast, his work seems to require a lot of additional breast contact, and I can smell scotch on his breath. I know the smell of Johnny Walker Red. I had downed several shots of it before this appointment.

Pain is present, but tolerable, like getting stung by a wasp or two regularly for about an hour. When the dentist is done, he reaches for some bandages. I look at the tattoo and am startled at how mushy it looks.

"Is that the way it should look?" I ask.

"Oh, yes, it will be fine."

He bandages the area. The tattoo stays covered for two days. When I unwrap it, the result is clear. The dentist did not color within the lines. Colors run together, there are no clear defining lines between the bloom and the stem.

I have a brightly colored blob on my breast. I can't stop my tears. I have hurt my own body. I don't want to call the dentist. In retrospect, he was creepy. And drunk. And besides, he's the one who screwed up. I call tattoo parlors to have it erased. They all say I cannot get rid of the little blob without extensive laser surgery that would result in a scar. I have to modify or add to it. The little rose would have to become something else.

I find a real tattoo artist about thirty miles away. She says she probably can work with the tattoo to fix it. She has a studio in her house so I still don't have to go into a tattoo parlor. I drive there, nervous and anxious. My trust instinct had been off with the last guy—what if it is still off?

The artist is middle-aged, a blowsy blond, sort of country. For some reason, that reassures me. She is what she is. She is not, like the dentist, one thing pretending to be another. I explain the problem with the dentist's tattoo. She doesn't hide her amusement.

"What the hell were you thinking goin' to a damn dentist for a tattoo? Girl, didn't you wonder why a dentist had to have a sideline?"

"Oh."

"What do you want me to make out of this mess?" she asks.

"Whatever makes sense to you," I respond, now completely intimidated. For the second time in a few short weeks, I am trusting a complete stranger with my body. "Just make it look good."

I am in the chair and she is working without excess breast touching.

"OK," I think, "this is going to turn out OK."

Then I notice a bulletin board on the wall directly in my line of sight. A Ku Klux Klan membership card is prominently displayed. I can feel my blood pressure rising. I am, after all, a civil rights lawyer. Oh my god. My brain reviews the damage she could do to my breast.

"Where do you work?" she asks.

Buzz, buzz goes the machine.

"For the government," I respond.

"What kind of work?"

"The Department of Education."

"What do you do there?"

Oh hell. I'm in it now. I take a deep breath.

"I'm a civil rights attorney."

The buzzing stops. My heart stops. There is a full ten seconds of silence.

"Well, fuck that," she says, and the buzzing begins again.

There is no more conversation. When the bees stop stinging me, she brings a mirror and holds it so I can see the tattoo. "What do you think?" she says.

I am now the proud owner of two roses, vines, leaves, and a butterfly. "I love it."

42

surprise

1992
age 51

I DON'T MOVE or open my eyes, waiting for the sounds to resolve, to be a passing car or some other city noise. Maybe it is my boyfriend making the noise. No, he is not here. He is closing his bar like every night. I wish he hadn't left after we argued. Tonight's argument was no worse than most.

There is the noise again. Louder. Damn. I hoped I imagined it or was dreaming. Now I am frightened. Something clearly is inside the house, maybe even in the room. Could be a rat. Or maybe someone has been watching the house and has broken in.

I keep my eyes tight shut. If I don't open them, nothing bad can happen. "Think good thoughts," I say silently. "There's nothing really wrong here, just some poor sick mouse . . . or rat.

Think happy thoughts. It is Christmas tomorrow. Nothing to be afraid of here."

The noises stop. I open my eyelids about a quarter inch. I'm on my side, facing the wall by the bed. There are flashing colored lights reflecting on the wall. "What?"

I roll over on my back as slowly and quietly as possible hoping not to distress the source of the sound. My eyes are still almost shut. Even through my lids, the lights are much brighter.

I gulp in air and sit up fast, wide-eyed, and ready to take on whatever monster has intruded.

In the far corner of the room is a naked man, adorned head to toe in red and green blinking Christmas lights. My boyfriend grins. "Merry Christmas!"

MOVING INWARD

secrets

"YOU KNOW DAD, with the exception of my husband, all men of interest to me have been Jewish. What do you make of that?"

"Oh, that's probably because my family was Jewish."

I must have misheard. I grew up in the Dutch Reformed Protestant church. My dad was an elder there.

"What? What did you just say?"

"Back in Germany, my family was Jewish."

"I know they were German, but Jewish?"

It is my mother who has begun to suffer dementia, not my father, yet I'm questioning what he is saying.

"Dad, are you sure about that?"

"Why wouldn't I be?"

"Your family was Jewish?"

"Yes."

"Dad, this doesn't sound right. Jewish? Then why aren't you Jewish? Why aren't I Jewish? Why aren't we *all* Jewish? What happened? How do Jews become Protestants? Did they become Protestant in Germany or what?" I know my questions are coming out too fast, but I can't stop. "What happened? When did it happen?"

My dad's voice is calm. His out-of-control eyebrows are knitted. Is he trying to remember? Could this be true?

"My Grandfather Maximillian was still Jewish when he came to America."

I want a cigarette but am afraid it will interrupt this incredible revelation.

"When did this happen?"

"In the 1880s, I think. Grandfather Max was just a teen-ager. He came with his older brother."

"They came by boat? Across the Atlantic?"

"It was a freighter. They just got on it somehow. Maybe they were working on it, I don't know. It stopped in New Jersey and Grandfather got off. He wasn't supposed to get off. The freighter was going on to South America."

MAXIMILLIAN AND MARIA RIST, 1896,
EAST RUTHERFORD, NJ; CATHOLIC AT THE TIME OF THEIR WEDDING.

"What happened to his brother?"

"He went with the freighter. Grandfather Max never heard from him again."

The facts are coming too fast for me to comprehend. My father is wheezing, breathless either from his asthma or from finally revealing this family secret.

"So, your grandfather came into this country illegally? And all by himself?"

"I guess."

"That was brave."

"Yes," says my father. "I think about that a lot."

"Why did he and his brother leave Germany?"

"My family's village was on the border between Germany and Poland. The village would change hands from time to time, and every time the Germans had it, there was some sort of purge or attack on the Jews who lived there. The brothers wanted out."

Dad is leaning forward in his chair looking at me with an uncharacteristic directness. I can tell he wants more questions.

"Why are you not Jewish? Why am I not Jewish?"

"I was told that when Grandfather Max hit the shore, he decided to become Catholic."

"He just *decided* that? You can't just *decide* to be a Catholic."

"Well, he did."

"Why Catholic?"

"I don't know if he wanted to be Catholic or just didn't want to be Jewish anymore."

"Did he really become Catholic? Did he go to church?"

"I know he did when he got married and had children. My mother told me."

"Dad, we are not Catholic."

"Right."

"How did we stop being Catholic? Did your grandfather just decide that too?"

"My mother told me that one day, when she was a little kid, the whole family was at mass. The priest started lecturing about insufficient money offerings. Grandfather Max had enough. He stood up, ordered the family to follow him, and marched out of the church. Then he became a Protestant. That's how we became Protestants."

Time for my cigarette. Time to re-enter the world I knew before this conversation, at least for a few minutes.

My mother is in the kitchen, setting the table for breakfast. I stop to say "Mom, Dad just said his family in Germany was Jewish. Can this be true?"

My mother doesn't stop what she is doing. She doesn't look at me.

"I guess it could be."

"*Could be?* Mom, how could I have never known about any of this? How come you and Dad never mentioned anything about this?"

She looks at me without expression. "The subject never came up."

addiction dance

I AM GENTLY rocking, lying in the bottom of a small rowboat.

"Whisper to yourself, 'I am happy and at peace.'"

"I am happy and at peace," I whisper.

"I do not want to drink alcohol."

I whisper that, too, although I'm not convinced it is true. How can it be true when I drink almost daily after work, either Johnny Walker Red or a bottle of wine. How could I suddenly not want to drink anymore?

"Alcohol of any kind tastes terrible."

"I will not drink alcohol again. I don't like it."

I do like it. I can go several days without drinking, but I always go back. It is impossible to have one drink, or two drinks. I'd love to give it up, but I don't think this is the way to do it.

I rock, pretending I believe hypnotism will work. A work friend commented on how much I was drinking. I was shocked. I thought nobody noticed.

If she saw a problem, did others? Were others just not saying so? Did my boss notice?

Has my work been affected?

The hypnotherapist is still giving me statements to repeat.

"Even the thought of alcohol makes me feel sick."

There are mornings when I can smell alcohol coming through my skin. There are mornings I don't make it to work.

I rock, whispering the phrases. Sometimes I can't tell whether I'm awake or asleep.

"You will wake up when I count to three."

I don't know how I can wake up when I think I have never been asleep.

"Three."

I sit up on the couch.

"I made a tape. Take it home and listen to it every night before you go to sleep. Or better yet, go to sleep listening to it. Come back next week and we will do it again."

My mind is at war with itself.

"She's a charlatan."

"No, she is saving my life."

"I don't believe in this stuff."

"But maybe it can work."

"Don't be stupid."

"Please let it work. Please."

45

shocker

1995
age 54

"WHY ARE YOU here?"

I don't want to answer the questions. I'm annoyed to be singled out from the fifty other students. I'm at this transformation workshop because I want to be. I was intrigued by their promised results. I planned to fly under the radar, just waiting for them to explain what they advertised so boldly: "You can become the sole, uncontested author of your life."

"Why are you here?"

"I was just curious. I don't need to be here."

"Why are you here? What are you pretending not to know?"

I need to give her an answer. I want the attention off me. My brain scatters, searching for an acceptable response.

"Sometimes I get overwhelmed." My voice is rising despite my attempts to keep it adult and even. "I have to stay strong all the time with my kids and my job and everything. I'm afraid . . . ."

Damn, why did I say that? I didn't mean to tell the truth.

"Are you willing to accept support?"

"I'm willing to consider advice."

"Not the same thing."

Scary thought.

"Do you know the definition of the word 'vulnerable'?"

"Yes, it means weak."

"Somebody get this woman a dictionary."

my brain

1995
age 54

I thank you my brain.
My friend, my defender, my protector, my guide.
You have brought me ideas, solutions, warnings, permissions.

You have stopped me when I approached danger,
You have alerted me when harm is near.
Your job is to protect me, to keep me safe.

But sometimes your protection stops me,
Your fear narrows my world, inhibits exploration,
lessens creativity.
Sometimes you prevent even love.

My world can embrace you yet entertain other,
You don't have to be my only tool.
Others are available, just new to me.

There is compassion, a way to bring others safely in,
There is awareness that I am not alone in the universe.
There is presence, that I am living right now, not dependent
on past or future.

Risk isn't always bad, change doesn't always hurt,
Love doesn't always wound.
And if it does, I won't die.

I love you my brain,
But now you are not the only game in town.

47

love

1996
age 55

"GIRLS, CAN WE talk?"

"Oh, for god's sake, do we have to do this?" asks my older daughter, J. "I don't like these *serious* talks."

"Yes, we do. I'm trying to ask for your forgiveness."

"Not necessary," says drama-averse J. "Now look what you are doing. L is already tearing up."

She is right. Younger daughter has tears threatening to spill.

"I want to ask you both if you can forgive me for letting you down as your mother. I love you and I know I didn't do a good job. I'm so sorry."

J's eyes roll. "Mom, get over yourself. We are in our thirties. It's over, it's done, it's fine."

"It's OK, Mom, it is," says L. "We forgive you. Lots of times I wished you were around more. I just missed you when you were out doing whatever you were doing."

"Yes."

"I know you feel bad about it," says L, "but we always knew we were loved. We know you love us. You were always hugging us and telling us how wonderful we were. We knew."

"Are we done?" asks J.

GOING OUT
WITH A BANG

48

without a net

1997
age 56

"WHY ARE YOU calling me in France? This must be important."

"I've been offered a new job," I say.

"Good for you. What is it?"

My friend doesn't seem surprised by the news, even though he knows I've been with the same agency doing civil rights work for almost twenty years.

"Chief of Staff of the International Broadcasting Bureau. Twenty thousand employees worldwide."

"Sounds great. When do you start?"

He is my left-brain friend. I have a tendency to jump. He is an analyzer, a critical thinker. I suspect he had a to-do list in his crib.

"Wait! I haven't decided. I don't know whether it would be right for me. And they want to know by tomorrow."

"Why not take the job?"

"I know nothing about international broadcasting. Absolutely nothing. The Director said it's a highly politicized agency focused on global politics. I don't think this is the place for on-the-job training."

"Then why did they offer you the job?

"The new director of the Bureau offered it because of the way I transformed one of the regional offices at the Office for Civil Rights."

"So, what's the problem? They know what they are getting."

"I ran an office of fifty people. Fifty! It's like they are asking the manager of a McDonald's to manage the food supply for the whole world. They can't be serious. I went through the interview for the job because I was flattered that I was even playing in this big arena."

"If they think you can do it, why don't you?"

This isn't what I was looking for. I wanted methods for decision-making. He, however, seems to have abandoned his left brain.

"There is no *right* decision here. You could put the names of your old agency and the new agency on the wall next to each other. Then throw a dart at the wall. Whichever one you hit will be the right one. It will be the right job because you will put your energy into it, so go throw a dart."

He sees I am afraid. I am about to leave the nest, my long-term secure job. I am about to jettison my best skills and knowledge for unknown territory. I could fail big time, and with a big audience.

I'd like to throw a dart at him.

49

we live in paradise

1998
age 57

THE TABLE IS laden with bowls of olives and feta cheese. The crusty bread sits next to the olive oil and tzatziki dip. Servers keep coming to the table with platters: fish, souvlaki, and other dishes I don't recognize. This tiny restaurant is hidden away on a back street on the beautiful Isle of Rhodes in the eastern Mediterranean. My dinner companions are six Greek union leaders, all male. I am here, in my new job in international broadcasting, to ease their fears about the imminent closing by the US government of the radio transmission station at which they work.

The men keep smiling and passing dishes to me. They all are unhappy that the facility where they work is going to be closed. I am the representative of the US government here to try to ease the blow by finding leads for other jobs for the soon-to-be displaced workers. I've been warned there might be aggressiveness against a government representative, particularly a female government representative, but so far all is friendly. If they are hoping to change the US government's mind about closing the plant by feeding me gloriously, I regret that I am going to disappoint them.

"But why are they closing the plant?" asks the union president.

Ah, we are down to business. Now I need to concentrate on the conversation, not the fabulous food.

"That answer is not really known to me. I know you are worried about your jobs. I'm here to help you find new jobs. We have some options for you."

"What?"

"Well," I say, "I spoke to the manager of the new Playboy Club being constructed here on the island. They will be needing some engineers and other tech people."

I hope they can't see how difficult it is for me to even *say* the words Playboy Club. "They will be opening within two months."

"That will only take care of the five or six of us that are highly skilled. What about the other twenty men who will be out of a job?"

I play my ace card.

"I've been working with the American Embassy. There are quite a number of job openings in Athens. We have spoken to several employers and they will be happy to accept applications and will give preference to you."

There is murmuring, in Greek, around the table. Even the waitress has joined in the talk. I don't understand a word.

The president hushes the others, then says, "You want us to leave paradise and move ourselves and our families to the armpit of Greece?"

"Well, that's where the jobs are!" I'm aware I sound defensive, but their reaction has surprised me. I thought they would be pleased about the jobs.

"Madam," says the president finally, "you don't understand what it means to have been born here, as was your mother and grandmother and great-grandmother. You don't understand our connection to this island. We live in paradise. We would rather starve here than live anywhere else."

PURE PLEASURE

50

gift for a guest

1998
age 57

WHITE WATER IS crashing over the front of the raft, momentarily blinding me. Paddler's screams are all I hear. I hope I am not screaming. I clench my toes in the foot strap, the only thing holding me in the raft. It's day nine of this two-week adventure, a retirement gift to myself.

We are finally safely through the Boucher and Crystal Creek rapids. I feel for the Kokopelli kachina figure I bought at a souvenir shop the night before we set out. Kokopelli is everywhere around this canyon. He has become my buddy. I always keep him close, whether in a pocket or in the bra top

of my bathing suit. He comforts me through rainy nights and raging rapids.

I am out of shape, new at rafting, and dislike camping. I am older than the other eleven paddlers and four guides. My arms, shoulders, and back ache from the unfamiliar paddling motion.

I'm living on ibuprofen.

It is the rainy season and I have been some degree of wet for nine days. I wear my bathing suit nine or ten hours a day, so I can slip over the edge of the raft to pee. The raft parade doesn't make rest stops.

My hips ache from sleeping on my side in a tiny tent with only a sleeping bag between me and a million tiny rocks. I woke up next to a rotting sheep head. Only the head. It had been dark when we pitched camp.

And yet—the trip is transformative. The physical aches and pains are present but irrelevant compared to the basalt gleam of the rock walls soaring above us, the sight of a bighorn sheep high above, climbing seemingly unclimbable walls, and the delicate golden flowers growing through cracks in rock. I am stilled by the silence of thousands of canyon years. I am a tiny figure, a guest here.

But now I am sitting on a rock, at river's edge, exhausted in mind, body, and spirit. The rest of the rafters have gone climbing up the canyon wall to see the Anasazi writings on the cliff face. The Anasazi lived on the canyon walls beginning around 500 AD. It was and is their canyon. My newly diagnosed lung condition has left me unable to make the climb. I am missing a once-in-a-lifetime opportunity. I sit in the sun; sad, tired, dispirited.

I pull Kokopelli out of my pocket. I hold him and close my eyes.

I hear flute music. It is floating down from the rock walls above me.

I stand and search the walls for the flute player but there is no one there. There is no one anywhere. There is only the music.

model behavior

I STAND ON the sidewalk, staring at the door of an old New York City warehouse. Rushing pedestrians swerve around me on their way to wherever. They make it clear I am in their way. I feel their baleful looks.

This can't be the right address. I double-check the piece of paper I wrote it on. Yes—this is it. Did I write it down wrong? Anxiety rises into my throat. It is 8:55 in the morning, and I am due at 9:00. Am I about to mess up my first ever modeling job? The instructions for the photo shoot just gave the name of the studio, J&H Productions, and the street address, but there are no names on the outside of this building.

It had seemed a great idea, post-retirement, to "model" that we can do anything at any age. I now am questioning my sanity.

I knock at the massive wooden door. This door is not going to be transmitting any messages. Even I, the one knocking, can't hear the knock. I try the door. It opens readily, as if it were expecting me. There is a handmade sign on the wall "J&H 3rd Floor." Many doors lead off this lobby-like area. Stairs may be behind one of them, but I don't have time to try them all. I see what looks like a freight elevator. I get into it even though I doubt the wisdom of doing this. There are no doors, only a rickety floor-to-ceiling gate to pull closed. I push the button for the third floor. The elevator lurches up in fits and starts. I pray it will make it, and I will live.

The elevator comes to a groaning stop at the third floor. It opens directly into an enormous loft space. Pop music is blaring. People are everywhere, and every one of them is doing something: moving, lifting, yelling instructions, steaming clothes, adjusting cameras and lights. It is an anthill of New Yorkers. I exit the elevator and stand just inside the loft, waiting for someone to notice. No one does.

I walk a few steps further into the space. No one sees me. No one says hello. Everyone just continues the dramatic action. I clear my throat, but just like knocking at that door, no one hears. Even when someone's eyes meet mine, they just slide on past and keep moving.

I am about to become the face of a product to strengthen old bones. I will be on all their national advertising. What's clear is that nobody in this building gives a damn.

I look around the room.

Several metal racks of clothes are standing next to each other on the back wall with a person fussing over them. I spot my picture hanging on the end of one of those metal racks. Thank god. I'm not in the wrong place or in a weird dream. I do exist. There I am. I go to the racks just as the person starts walking away. "Wait! I'm here. I'm Jean."

I point to my picture in case my words aren't enough.

"Yeah, and?"

"Well, I'm here."

"I saw you. You're the talent."

"I am?"

"Yeah." He points to my photo. "You're her."

"Yes."

"So, what do you want?"

"I don't know what I'm supposed to do."

EVISTA offers proven fracture risk reduction
For the prevention and treatment of osteoporosis in postmenopausal women

EVISTA significantly reduces risk of
<u>first</u> vertebral fracture.[1]

EVISTA is an excellent choice

MORE Trial Demographic Data

Trial Size	7,705 postmenopausal women
Mean T-scores at initiation of trial[2]	-2.6 at the spine
	-3.2 at the femoral neck
Length of trial	36 months
Mean age of participants[1]	67 years
All participants were provided	calcium (500 mg/day)
	vitamin D (400–600 IU/day)

See pages 12-13 for important safety information and references;
see pages 14-19 for prescribing information for EVISTA.

"Go to hair and makeup. Jeez, you never done this before?"

"Actually, no, I haven't."

"Well, get moving."

New Yorkers.

I head in the direction he pointed for hair and makeup. These folks are friendly and I get more comfortable in the space. It is fantasy fulfillment to have my hair and makeup done.

I'm directed back to wardrobe where I try on four different outfits until the wardrobe guy is happy.

Now it is time for the actual photo shoot. I stand in front of a blank paper backdrop. The photographer is female. This makes me more comfortable, maybe she isn't judging me as much as a male would. I stand there smiling at the camera.

"Can you move a little?" requests the photographer.

"Move where?"

"No, not 'move where'—I mean move your body."

"Really?"

I want to say, "But these are still shots."

"Yes, walk forward a step or two, jump up, throw your arms in the air, strike a pose . . . anything!"

I regret not learning how to be a model before I became one.

"I'm sorry," I say. "I didn't know I was supposed to do that."

"Have you done this before?" she asks.

"No. This is my first time."

"Aha," she says. "Wait just a minute."

The photographer disappears. Suddenly Madonna is now blasting from the speakers with "Like a Virgin."

She comes back laughing. "Is that better? Feel more comfortable?"

"Oh yes."

I start moving.

the day of betty friedan

2001
age 60

I DON'T HAVE the clout to invite national powerhouses to come on my new little internet radio show. A friend says, "Why don't you invite Betty Friedan to be interviewed on 'Women of a Certain Age'? She's old, she lives here in DC, and I think she is bored."

Bored? How can she be bored? She wrote the ground-breaking book *The Feminine Mystique*, catapulting the modern feminist movement into being.

Why would she agree to come on this little show? Betty Friedan is known worldwide, founding or co-founding organizations like NOW and the Women's Political Caucus. She is one complicated woman: a visionary, but a difficult and argumentative person who either left, or was helped to exit, essentially every organization she founded.

Ms. Friedan agrees to the interview. I am to pick her up and transport her to and from the radio studio. Her assistant also gives me permission to call Ms. Friedan 'Betty.' I'm not sure I can do that.

Today is the day. I drive to Ms. Friedan's beautiful art deco apartment building in DC. She lives alone on the top floor. I am intimidated. I go in. I go up. I knock. Ms. Friedan's assistant answers the door. She leads me to a sitting room and says, "Betty will come when she is ready."

I am so nervous about meeting the icon. I take in nothing about the room except that it is stifling hot, which increases my discomfort.

A half hour passes with no sound coming from anywhere in the apartment. Then the icon in question walks in. My expectation was a giant of a woman. She cannot be more than five feet tall, if that. Her body is tiny. It also is engulfed in a full-length mink coat, with matching fur hat. "I'm ready," she says. No introduction, no how are ya.

"I'm Jean Peelen," I say, "and I am honored to meet you, Ms. Friedan."

"Yes." She heads for the door.

The ride from DC to the studio in Virginia, normally twenty minutes without traffic, today drags on for forty-five minutes. There is almost no conversation.

"How are you? Are you comfortable?"

"Turn on the heat."

OK. It is May and she is in full fur. Sweat is running down my back.

"We're almost there."

Nothing.

We arrive at the tiny recording studio. She stares in what only can be dismay. Is she thinking, "Lord, how I have fallen"?

She squeezes into the booth and sits down on the folding chair. I fit the earphones on her and close the studio door to block out street noise. The temperature must be eighty degrees. She is still in full fur gear.

I begin the interview. For the first four or five questions she answers simply "yes" or "no." My heart is sinking. This is no interview. The woman does not want to be here and could not give a damn about who I am, or what I'm trying to do. This is not personal. She just doesn't care.

Finally, I say in a loud voice surprising even to me, "Betty! This is a participatory activity. Please participate!"

For the first time since she walked into the room in her apartment, she looks at me. Her eyes focus.

"What do you want?"

"Betty, in five or less words, why did you write *The Feminine Mystique*?"

"Because I was miserably unhappy."

Thank you god. Now I can really begin the interview. I ask about her life, about the content of *The Feminine Mystique*. She notes that when women were pulled out of the factories and sent home after World War II, they suffered depression, forced back into their former tiny worlds. It was proof to her that we women were not made to inhabit just the four walls of our husbands' houses, and if forced to do so, depression, sickness, and even addictions are the result.

Her memory is sharp, and she thinks clearly.

It is a wonderful interview, and I am in the presence of a great woman.

après interview

BEFORE I DRIVE Betty home, I ask offhandedly if she would like to see the log cabin I am in the process of buying in Alexandria.

"Sure," she says.

We drive to my cabin, Betty now talking nonstop like we are old friends. I don't mind in the least that it is not a two-way conversation. I am listening to a historical figure tell me about her life and times.

She loves my rustic, tiny cabin, and she really loves the little out-building that sits on the bank of a stream. "You are going to write here," she says.

"No," I reply. "I work for the government. I write legal memos about civil rights."

"No," she says. "You are going to write here."

54

american gothic

2003
age 62

I TURN INTO the short driveway to the independent living facility. I see the two figures sitting on the bench outside of the office, backs straight, holding hands. It is my parents. They are looking for me but don't see me inside the unfamiliar rental car.

They are, as always, in their own world, their own bubble of love. My mom is in a pink print top and pink polyester knit pants, her lipstick perfectly matching her pants. My dad is in his usual shorts and fisherman cartoon T-shirt, 123 pounds soaking wet but with the tiniest of paunches. Their feet, clad in matching white sneakers, mirror their hands, touching each other.

It is so odd to see my parents as a painting, as eternal. The anxiousness on my mom's face is centered on my imminent arrival. I know it will disappear as soon as they see me.

granddaughters

2004
age 63

MARCH FOR WOMEN'S Lives, Washington, DC.

How proud I am. How proud of my daughters, how proud of my granddaughters, all marching with me.

COSTS

56

—————

unlicensed

—————

2006
age 65

I CALL THE Florida DMV to take my parents' driver's licenses away.

"Do you think they are a danger on the road?" asks the DMV person.

"Well, my father can't remember where he is going, and my mother has forgotten the rules of the road. On my last visit, my mom drove us to the grocery store. We came to a stop sign. Mom stopped. A car was coming on the cross street. Mom started up again into its path. I shrieked and she stopped."

"Did she not see the other car?"

"She saw it. She told me that once she stops at a stop sign, she can go again and it is up to everyone else to look out for her."

The clerk says they will approve taking their licenses away.

"And this is anonymous, right? They won't know who called them?"

"Absolutely."

Nothing happens for over a year. No DMV activity. My sisters and I come up with a plan. I convince my parents that because they hardly ever drive anywhere, and because the retirement community has vans to take them to Publix, Walmart, and church, it would be a loving thing for them to give their car to their Michigan daughter. The plan works. My sister flies down and gets the car. We all breathe a sigh of relief.

Then my mother calls me. She is very angry.

"Jean, somebody came to our door. They said they were from the Florida Department of Motor Vehicles, and they came to get our driver's licenses."

"What?" I feel my insides gripping. I am prepared to lie my way out of this.

"They said you reported us to them. You told them to come get our licenses."

Oh hell.

"They really said that? They said my name?" I ask, wavering between pretending outrage at a false allegation and admitting it. I need to stall for time.

"They said it was a daughter so it was one of you three. We figured it probably was you. How dare you do that to us. How *dare* you! You had no right to do that."

"Oh, Mom, I am so sorry. We were all worried about you two. We were so afraid you would get into an accident, or you would get lost and someone would take advantage of you because of your age."

"We are your parents! You had no right to make that decision. Your father and I are very angry with all of you. Shame on you."

No one wants to hear that from a parent. No one. And no parent wants to hear their children deem them incapable of taking care of their own lives. There is pain on both sides.

I begin crying. "Mom, I am so sorry. I am so sorry. We were just trying to do what we thought best. If we did wrong, I am so sorry."

"You made up a whole story about your sister needing a car! You tricked us." Half not true, half true.

"No, Mom, she did badly need a car. That was true. You really helped her when she needed it."

"Oh, Jean," her voice softening. "We wanted to help her, but you all should not have called the state to come get our driver's licenses. It was awful."

"I'm so sorry. They actually took your licenses away?"

"Yes, they demanded we give them to them. I told them it was our only form of ID, but they didn't care."

"Oh, that's terrible. We will get you some other form of ID."

Up to this point, my mother is speaking completely clearly and rationally, so much so that I am thinking maybe the dementia isn't so bad. Maybe we acted precipitously. Maybe I am a bad daughter.

"Oh no," says Mom. "You don't have to worry about our ID. We took care of that."

"How?"

"We told them that before we gave them our licenses, we had to cut out our photos from them so that we could show people and they would know who we are. We cut out our pictures, and we carry them in our wallets."

invisible no more

THE LIBRARY MEETING room in Sag Harbor is filling with women in their seventies, eighties, and perhaps their nineties. We three authors are used to presenting our just published book, *Invisible No More: The Secret Lives of Women Over 50,* to women in their forties and fifties.

We present the issues of being over fifty with our usual pizzazz and humor.

"Our bodies are beginning to sag, bag, and drag."

"Nobody seems to see us anymore, men don't stare, or even glance. Clerks at the cosmetics counter overlook us."

We talk about the renewed energy we discovered after fifty, what an NPR reviewer called "post-menopausal zest." Our children are raised, our careers are complete, and we are blessed with good-enough health.

The women in the audience all listen closely to our tales of menopause, of breast cancer, of sex, of facelifts, of romance. Then comes the Q&A session.

"I'm sorry, dear. What you've said is all very interesting, but your issues aren't our issues. Our issues are that our bodies are falling apart in every possible way, our families are mostly all dead, and our friends are dying at a great rate. I don't know how to get past those things with the positive thinking you rate so highly."

Oh. We are without funny comebacks; in fact, we are without speech. We smile, nod, and say we understand. Yet I can feel something within shrinking away from this unwanted information. I don't want to hear. I don't want to know. I want to get out of this room as soon as possible.

Joyce Kramer • Renee Fisher • Jean Peelen

INVISIBLE
NO MORE:

The Secret Lives of Women Over 50

"For these three brave women, life began at 50 years of age
when they made a decision to be honest about themselves.
Thankfully, they have shared their stories with us."
—Betty Friedan, author of *The Feminine Mystique*

the rest is still unwritten

2006
age 65

I WASN'T EXPECTING her to look like she did. She is my younger sister. I have known her for fifty-seven years. She is standing in my hotel lobby, very short bright blue sundress, high heels, and bruises covering almost every inch of her exposed body. People are staring, trying not to be caught at it.

My sister is dying.

I stare at her, trying to understand what I am seeing. Her dress is hanging on her frame.

Her face, despite the blazing red lipstick, is drawn and pale.

Nothing is right in the way she looks, yet she stands tall, looking around the lobby like she owns it.

I know her breast cancer has recurred. I was with her three years ago when she went to the hospital for a routine lumpectomy; instead, a much larger, malignant tumor was found. The doctor said an immediate mastectomy was imperative.

I was with her when she woke up to find her breast gone. She was inconsolable and angry.

"But I didn't get to say anything! I didn't get to say whether I wanted them to take it."

"But," said the practical me, "there was no choice. Your doctor said it had to happen."

"I don't care!" she screamed. "How could you let that happen?"

How indeed? Her husband consoled her and affirmed it was he who made the decision. She did not want to forgive either of us.

She went through two difficult years of chemo and radiation and then into remission. She finally got her life back on track and discovered her calling as a salesperson. Then the cancer came back, aggressive, metastasized, and stage four.

She has again been undergoing chemo and even more heavy-duty radiation treatments. She had told me the radiation was causing bruising, but I had had no idea the extent of it.

I am in Chicago as a volunteer to recruit women into an NIH breast cancer study, the Sister Study, because both of my sisters have now had breast cancer. I was annoyed that my younger sister asked to drive over from Michigan to spend the night with me. She has always been an annoying sister: loud, dramatic, profane, wears shorts that show her ass, has led a life that caused damage and destruction. She drinks too much and has flirted with drug addiction.

She sees me and flies across the lobby to hug me, as usual, in the most flamboyant way possible. I laugh because she is drama as usual, but tears are threatening. I can feel her sharp bones as we hug. What is it like to be dying? Does she know?

We go up to my room and sit on the bed and talk. We haven't done this in many years. An actual sister talk. We hug again, which hasn't happened with real feeling, with love, in forever. She starts talking about how much she relishes her job, and what she sees in her future. So, she doesn't know. Or is this bravado?

In the middle of a sentence, she interrupts herself to exclaim: "I have a great new favorite song. You have to hear it."

I don't care to hear it; I'm trying to hold myself together. I want, I so want, to deny facts.

"It's called 'Unwritten.'"

"I don't care about a song right now."

"Sit down and listen."

I surrender.

"Future . . . Who knows? What now? Unwritten . . . " The meaning of the song knifes through my brain.

My sister knows she is dying.

the nursing home

2008
age 67

I MAKE THE dreaded journey. It is on the calendar every month, but sometimes I stretch it to every other month. I get increasingly anxious on the plane. Duty has called me here, and duty will get me through it. The plane sets down in Ft. Lauderdale just two hours from the snow in Virginia. I wonder what it would be like to be coming for lazy days at the beach.

The rental car company is the cheapest available. Sometimes they can't produce a car and sometimes I have to wait for one. I don't mind. The waiting delays seeing Mom. I sit on the cracked plastic chair in the rental office.

Dad has been gone for a year. He and Mom were separated at the nursing home in his last days. Mom would wander the halls looking for him and calling his name. She barely remembers him now. For sixty-nine years, they held each other's hands everywhere they went; first for love, then for stability of walking, and finally because my mother didn't know where she was going without him. Mom now sleeps at least eighteen hours a day. She recognizes no one but the aide she sees every day.

Alzheimer's was Mom's biggest fear. Her mother had it for the last ten years of her life. Mom cared for her mother, first at home, then every day in the nursing home. Mom hated her own failing memory, her inability to remember words. She fretted that maybe she had developed Alzheimer's. We all denied it and reassured her she was just fine, that it was just age at work.

But we were lying.

I thought it healthier for her to know what was happening to her, so I convinced Dad to tell her the truth.

Dad told Mom she has Alzheimer's. She refused to believe it and was enraged with him for suggesting it. They argued. Dad was shaken.

"I will never do that again," he said. "It is our rule that we say 'I love you' every night before we go to sleep. Last night your mother turned her back on me. I'm going to tell her I was mistaken about the Alzheimer's."

I drive the ten miles to the nursing home, slower than I ever drive, anxiety making me inattentive. I dread, yet again, to see my once capable, determined mother in her current state of semi-consciousness. I park and sit in the car wishing to be anywhere but here. I pray for strength, take a deep breath, and walk into the building. I am hit with that horrible, never-to-be-forgotten smell of decay, urine, and death. It is always thus.

I walk the long hall and stop in front of Mom's room, unwilling to open the door and feel my own anguish. I go in only because an aide is coming down the hall. Mom is sleeping, facing away from me. I want to wait a minute before touching her, but she rolls over and opens her eyes. I don't know how she knows anyone is here. She is deaf and her hearing aids are constantly lost. She stares at me. What is she seeing? Who does she think I am?

She focuses. "Jean, is that you or am I dreaming?"

60

---

shadow

2017
age 76

My mother fought Alzheimer's.
My grandmother died of it.
Will I? Will I?

Am I running from the already written?
Am I just a few steps ahead?
Is the curse inevitable?

I flex my brain to its limits.
I read, I research, I learn.
I wish to stay sane.

My grandmother began at eighty.
My mother around the same age.
Eighty is rushing toward me.

I imagine, I create, I fret.
I walk, I study, I take THC.
And finally accept whatever is to be.

I am a creature of the universe.
I will or won't become demented.
I claim every minute as my last.

AND THE
BEAT GOES ON

61

beautiful island

2014
age 73

EVERY SEAT IS filled in the Holmes Beach, Florida, City Hall, and people are standing, leaning against the walls. The city auditorium is a sea of yellow T-shirts proclaiming, "Protect Our Builders!" In the front row is the biggest developer on the island, his lawyer next to him. Smugness radiates from them.

A tall man slips quietly into the auditorium and moves to a far back corner. Most of the audience is facing forward and don't see him, but from the dais, the sight is startling. On an island where flip-flops and T-shirts are the norm, he blares his presence with black suit, black shirt, black tie, black wrap-around shades. He stands unmoving, legs slightly spread and hands clasped loosely in front of him. Is he here to kill me or save me?

I look sideways at my fellow city commissioners on the dais. This undoubtedly is the most dramatic situation they have ever experienced. They are frozen in their chairs, microphones turned off.

I am the cause of this mess. I thought I was moving to this peaceful, sweet, little island to really, *really* retire. But I got bored. I ran for office because I saw an election for the Holmes Beach City Commission was about to occur. I'd never experienced elective office, so why not?

I campaigned by knocking on doors and talking with people. That's when I got educated to the ongoing destruction of the community. The island is sweet, and it is little, but the developers have gotten hold of it.

Decades-old beach cottages are being demolished and replaced by six-, eight-, even ten-bedroom houses. These houses are rented out weekly for megabucks. Neighborhoods are no longer neighborhoods. They are just streets of short-term rental houses.

Couples retire to their dream beach cottage only to have the cottages on either side of them torn down and replaced

★ A New Voice ★

ELECT **Jean Peelen**

for Holmes Beach City Commissioner

http://www.youtube.com/user/JeanPeelen

Political advertisement, paid for and approved by Jean Peelen for Holmes Beach Commission

with three-story monster houses. Every week, twelve to twenty short-term renters move into these houses, bringing noise, traffic, and trash with them. The retirees flee. They sell their cottages to live peacefully somewhere else. Down goes yet another cottage, and in its place comes another mega-house. It is classic blockbusting for the economics of tourism.

I take several deep breaths. Tonight I will present my report "Crisis in Holmes Beach," laying out the issues that our community is being destroyed by uncontrolled development. I now also know our building department has been complicit in the process. The other Commissioners got an advance copy of the report.

Word of the presentation clearly has been conveyed to the builder community. Thus the presence of all these yellow shirts. The commission chair, great friends with the developer, begs, pre-meeting, for me to *not* read the report aloud.

I decline the request.

Public Comment occurs at the beginning of the meeting, so I haven't yet presented the report. Speaker after speaker from the audience declares I am ruining their income and thus their families by promoting restrictions on building. The developer's attorney is the last speaker in the long line of citizens making public comments.

"The restrictions you are putting on the size and shape and occupancy of rental houses are not legal. They restrain trade and deny builders the right to create the highest use of the land. Your proposed rules will result in a flood of lawsuits."

He concludes with, "And let me remind you there may be suits against one or more commissioners in their personal capacity." Although he is speaking to the whole commission, he looks only at me. This threat is not a surprise. I already have been sued by one such developer and am frightened by it.

Several police officers appear at the back of the auditorium. Someone must have called them. They seem laser-focused on the dark stranger in the corner. I don't know if that is good or bad. Who is he?

I search the crowd for friendly faces. Here's one, there's another, but they are greatly outnumbered by my critics. In the front row is a friendly face. She sits right next to the developer, seemingly immune to him, his political pull, his charms, his money, or his attorney. It is she who anonymously performed the research for my report documenting the destruction of the community. She is deadly serious about protecting the island. Her parents built the house she inherited from them. Just looking at her gives me courage.

I realize she is without her husband who normally sits next to her. He is a retired homicide detective from New Orleans. I wonder why he is not in his place. Then I get it. He is standing in the back.

tiny living

2018
age 77

THE WOMAN PULLS her lumbering old dog to a halt. "Hi—you're new here, right?"

"Yes, just moved in a few weeks ago."

"From Florida? For some reason, everybody moves here either from Vermont or Florida."

"Florida. I couldn't stand the heat or the tourists anymore."

"Yup, I saw them bringing in your tiny house about a month ago. It's a nice one. Do you know which builder built your house? There are differences in quality, you know. Are you having the front porch screened? Are you having a back porch built on?"

I squirm at this degree of neighbor interaction. In my old condo in Florida, only one other person lived in my building year-round. Other than saying hello if we crossed paths, I didn't know her. In this North Carolina tiny house village, every day is a dog parade, with over-fifty folks traipsing around the village and gathering in little groups to chat.

The woman's dog strains at the leash, anxious for the dog park.

"Yes, I like it so far."

"Do you have any questions? Anything I can help you with?"

I decide to shock her. "Yes, do you know how to get a prescription for marijuana in North Carolina? I am unfamiliar with the rules here about marijuana."

"Why would you need a prescription?"

"Because it's illegal? But I read that THC could stave off Alzheimer's."

"It is illegal. There are no exemptions for medical marijuana in this state, but there are a couple of folks here in the village that can get it for you. I can ask one to get in touch with you."

"What? There are drug dealers here?"

She laughs. "OK, if that's how you see it. Most of us are over fifty with accompanying aches and pains. Some of us just want to get high, like having a drink before dinner. Some of us want to sleep better."

"Yes, please. I would like to have someone contact me."

pandemic insanity

2020
age 79

"SO WHAT IS keeping you busy?" asks my ever-supportive friend.

"There's a pandemic."

"Well, yes, but what are you doing? What's your vision for your life?"

That "vision" question has been going back and forth between us for years. Sometimes we are joking, sometimes not.

"What is anybody's purpose right now?"

"Come on, quit stalling. I know you've been staying home like we all have, but what is your vision for right now?"

"Mostly I've been feeling old. I have started writing again though."

"What are you writing?"

"I guess it's a memoir, but mostly it's just random stuff from my life. I do have an idea about something else I want to do."

"What?"

"I'm going to get a facelift."

She laughs. We've had the vanity/surgical help talk numerous times. She is against it. I am for it.

"No, seriously, what's your vision?"

"I've found a surgeon and am scheduled to have a facelift in December."

"Why? Why? Why would you do such a thing, and for god's sake, why in the middle of a pandemic?"

"I'm bubbling with other ideas, too. I want to get a different president elected. I want to improve at Pilates. I want to take writing courses. I want to start a writer's group. I want to write that memoir."

"You can't do all that without having a facelift?"

"I want to look good. I want to look alive and vibrant."

"You know I think this is a stupid idea, and really stupid mid-pandemic."

"Go ahead and say it: I am overly concerned with looks. I am too vain."

"I don't have to state what you already believe. Hard as it is to say though, I think you should do what makes you your best self, whatever that means to you."

I love you, friend.

roe v. *wade*

2022
age 81

I WAVE MY protest sign at the passing cars, looking for thumbs up or honks of acknowledgment. Why am I *still* doing this?

In the 1960s, I waved "Our bodies our choice" signs in Alabama.

In the 1970s, I waved them in Washington, DC.

In 1973, *Roe* v. *Wade* was decided. That ruling guaranteed we could now and forever make our own choices about our own bodies. We thought we had created a gift for our children and our children's children.

In 2004, tens of thousands of women gathered when the then-president threatened our right to choose. Again, I waved that sign. It was the first I realized our rights were not guaranteed forever.

In 2022, *Roe* v. *Wade* is no more the law of the land and abortion is criminalized.

These are our bodies. Will we never again make our own decisions about them?

I wave my sign. I am eighty-one years old. I will wave. I will wave the damned signs. It is what I do.

and now

2023
age 82

And now I am eighty-two and looking back.
So much joy, so much suffering.
Lessons lost and learned.

In my view from now old bones,
I see the suffering as needless.
Just a gift from a woman-controlling world.

So many years of guilt for negligent mothering.
Says who?
Those who would keep us in the house.

My children suffered too,
Caught in the same paradigm.
Now I finally see the construct.

It will always be a fight for us,
And none will be free until all are.
Freedom should not come at such cost.

Thank you to the women who cut a path to follow.
Thank you to those now showing the way.
And fight, my granddaughters, fight to fly.

acknowledgments

IT DID, INDEED, take a village—a women's village—to complete this book. I simply could not have done it alone.

Kimberly Tyler was my editor throughout the writing of *Feisty*. I am so grateful. I was the *David* to her Michelangelo, an unformed newbie, an insecure writer. She took me from being a writer who felt it necessary to "drive the point home" to one who began to understand subtlety, who began to respect her readers. She never wrote or changed writing. She simply asked questions, and that made all the difference.

Susan Aitel, my old work companion, premier proofreader, and all-around lovely person, was tireless in championing *Feisty*. She read, read, and re-read. She caught every change I made or should have made. I am so grateful.

My dearest and oldest friend Deborah Ashford, a consistent source of love, encouragement, and great ideas.

My several friends—Maggie, Joyce, Gail, Joanne, Michelle, Camille, Whitney, MaryLou—who read early drafts and gave nonstop encouragement.

My writer friends, Jill Nelson, Alison Acheson, Heather Newton, Jane Campbell, and Liz Tigelaar who read drafts and sent lovely blurbs and encouragement.

Daughter Lisa who never read the whole manuscript but exactly understood what I was up to and gave great feedback on individual chapters; and daughter Jennifer who also did not read it but said "Mom, say anything you want to say. It's your truth." Thank you both.

Thank you to my publisher Bold Story Press founder and CEO Emily Barrosse; editor Karen Gulliver who first read and championed *Feisty*; Julianna Scott Fein, production editor who kept everything moving; and cover and interior designer Karen Polaski. I am grateful.

about bold story press

BOLD STORY PRESS is a curated, woman-owned hybrid publishing company with a mission of publishing well-written stories by women. If your book is chosen for publication, our team of expert editors and designers will work with you to publish a professionally edited and designed book. Every woman has a story to tell. If you have written yours and want to explore publishing with Bold Story Press, contact us at https://boldstorypress.com.

**BOLD
STORY
PRESS**

The Bold Story Press logo, designed by Grace Arsenault, was inspired by the nom de plume, or pen name, a sad necessity at one time for female authors who wanted to publish. The woman's face hidden in the quill is the profile of Virginia Woolf, who, in addition to being an early feminist writer, founded and ran her own publishing company, Hogarth Press.

Printed in Great Britain
by Amazon